SPINE

Cynthia Roses-Thema

SPINE:

5 Somatic Strategies for 21st Century Dancers

by

Cynthia Roses-Thema, Ph.D.

Turning Point Press

2016

SPINE*: 5 Somatic Strategies for the 21st Century Dancer*

Published by TurningPointPress 2016
PO Box 81, Teaneck, NJ 07666
turningpointpress@gmail.com

© 2015 by Cynthia Roses-Thema
Cynthia Roses-Thema portrait photograph © Graham Thema

ISBN 978-0-9908556-7-5 (**Trade Paperback $39.95**)
ISBN 978-0-9973829-1-4 (**eBook $27.95**)

Also available:

SPINE: Using the SPINE Strategies in Contemporary Ballet (SPINE Workbook)
ISBN 978-0-9908556-8-2 (**Trade Paperback $34.95**)
ISBN 978-0-9973829-2-1 (**eBook $24.95**)

SPINE Strategies & Workbook Set
(Available in hardcopy only from www.turningpointpressllc.com) $60.00

Cover design by Cynthia Roses-Thema
Layout design by David Bass

To all my amazing and wonderful students

SPINE: 5 SOMATIC STRATEGIES
TABLE OF CONTENTS

Preface

The five strategies that comprise my **SPINE** are my life's work. I created these strategies when I began to teach ballet after finishing my career as a professional ballerina. I continued to experiment with these strategies when I went on to have my own studio and direct and choreograph for my own company. I brought my SPINE strategies to the university where I currently teach. Everywhere I have taught these strategies students can do more with the body with less injury, less pain and it takes less time to learn the moves. And further these strategies work for a wide variety of populations. But I'm getting ahead of myself here. In this preface I would like to tell you the story of how these five strategies were born.

I was teaching dance at Southern Ballet Theatre in Orlando, Florida. I didn't want to tell my students what the body needed to look like in movement; I wanted to direct them to what the body felt like in movement. It was a totally different approach to ballet – trying to tell dancers what movement felt like, but I believed strongly it was what was needed to prevent injury and empower my students. That's why on a sunny day in Orlando, Florida I sat in my living room with my dictionary open. What words could I use to describe to my students what I felt in my body as I danced?

I had found in my professional career that teacher's, choreographer's or director's comments came most often from the observed perspective (their perspective of watching me dance) and directed me to what my body needed to look like. In addition I would get feedback about specific body parts like "Don't sickle your foot" or "Keep your hip down." As I tried to achieve these goals, I remember the specific parts of my body blowing up in my imagination and I lost the connections in my body. The consequence of trying to operate my body from an observed perspective was that I operated my body by saying never mind how the movement felt, just get it right.

But just getting it right I found led to three more errors in my movement somewhere else because I was forcing and not working my body in a healthy way. I didn't want injuries. To date I have none. I have had no surgeries, no major problems during the ten years I danced professionally. Why? I believe it was because I had achieved my own way of physically sensing my whole body as I moved to create technique from my own perspective. But I had never told anyone what I was sensing or even tried to express it to myself – it was always just what I felt. Now I was teaching others and I wanted to teach them technique from this physical, personal and experiential perspective! What to do? How to put my beliefs into action?

I stood up in my living room and extended my arms sideways. I felt stretch in my body, a length. I realized my moving body never felt crunched or bunched up when I danced. I had been a Harkness trainee under the direction of David Howard and Maria Vegh and I knew there could be scientific principles and ideas applied to the moving body. I didn't have to rely on luck or chance. I had built my ability to sense my body during movement on a very scientific foundation during my professional career.

So why not resort to a scientific approach and just use a simple word like stretch I said to myself? I looked up stretch in the dictionary: elastic was described as stretch. Yes, that word described well what I was sensing – an elasticity not just an extension outward but a give and take in my limbs. It also wasn't just a stretch throughout the body. Instead I sensed there were pathways where I felt the stretching, so a directional element was there. What about the word road? Stretch Road? Yes, that would work. The idea of a road having movement in two directions also connected to the idea that when I did extend my arms to the side there was a give and take to the experience. I sensed a stretch outwards, but also a sense of a stretch coming into and through my torso that connected one arm to the other.

What next? The floor. I danced on a floor. What was my contact with the floor? I stood in a first position. I sensed myself press into the floor. Then I moved my arms, but I also felt myself press into the air. Pressing the Floor and Air – what about pressing flair?

I had **S** for *stretch roads* and **P** for *pressing flair*. What next? What else did I sense during movement?

I could dance with great speed but in that speed there was a lightness; a sense of being able to move great distances with minimal effort. Minimal effort? I did the *"chicken step"* from Balanchine's *Concerto Barocco* – a piece that required incredible speed. I felt economical when I did this step. I decided on the verb *economizing* to indicate that there was an efficiency in how the body could travel far without tensing and/or gripping. Okay, so I had an **S**, a **P**, and an **E**.

I realized these three words didn't describe everything I felt though, and I couldn't just have a bunch of words to explain to my students. I needed something that would help them remember these ideas and would give a lot of information in just a single word. A **mnemonic** was what I wanted.

It took me a week or so to figure out the word I would use was **SPINE** with each letter standing for a different strategy.

The **N** was difficult, but I finally settled on the term *neutralizing* and that for me explained the sense of the joints in the body being opened with equal push outwards so that there was a sense of the pull/push of the joints all being neutral. Neutralizing joint points became a strategy that connected to controlling the body by maintaining connections to the centers of the body as the body went from shape to shape. Neutralizing joint points also justified the use of turnout and helped with creating the torque for turns.

I decided the **I** in **SPINE** would stand for *interpreting* and that is a strategy I am very proud of because the **SPINE** strategies for moving the body also connect technique to the artistry of dance. And that is something that other ways of explaining or dealing with technique don't do — other strategies don't explain the technique of artistry. Artistry is not a gift, but a skill that can be achieved through interpreting movement.

That's how the **SPINE** strategies were born.

Why introduce them to you now? Well, I see a real need for the SPINE strategies as a way for dancers to understand how to move the body because I see the story of dance itself changing.

Dance used to be very strict in terms of what each genre was. Ballet looked like ballet and had certain characteristics. Modern had another set of characteristics; jazz and tap the same. A dancer used to be able to just be proficient in one genre and that was enough. All that began to change when I was dancing professionally in the late 1970s and 1980s.

I became a professional ballet dancer at age 17 when I was hired by the *Chicago Ballet Company* where I stayed and worked my way through the ranks to ballerina in five years. Then I went to the *Cincinnati Ballet Company* as a ballerina and stayed there for another five years.

I created over 60 roles in my career everything from the traditional classic ballet roles of *Sugar Plum Fairy* and *Odette* in *Swan Lake* to, at that time, Minsa Craig's totally avant garde work, *November Steps*.

Along the way, I performed Balanchine's contemporary ballets and many of Ruth Page's works such as *Frankie and Johnny,* a jazzy Americana ballet based on the ballad "Frankie and

Johnny." I've done the modern works of Richard Arve, Lar Lubovitch, Lester Horton, Doris Humphrey, as well as *Flying Home*, a swing dance/jitterbug work of Lois Bewley.

My point is, my one body had to perform a variety of different dance genres. While I was dancing professionally the boundaries between the dance genres were slowly dissolving. Now, in the 21st century, the story of dance is not just about being versatile but about mixing and matching steps from dance genres. Choreography is a hybridization of movement. Some call it movement fusion.

The consequence of such hybridization in choreography for 21st century dancers means there is a need to have an increased focus for the dancer on sensing his/her body during movement. The story of dance in the 21st century is the story of knowing one's body so well during movement that any move is possible!

Possibilities are one of the main focuses of the SPINE strategies I've created. And these possibilities are brought into the light and made explicit because the SPINE gives names to what the dancer senses during movement. The inner perspective of what the dancer feels is in some ways a territory yet to be made explicit because there are no words to describe what the dancer senses during movement. The SPINE strategies change that. These strategies give voice by naming sensations of what the dancer experiences during movement.

Now at this point you might be a bit skeptical. How can these strategies work for me you ask? But I would like you to know that I have tried and tested the SPINE strategies on thousands of dancers over a fifteen-year period. And these strategies work on dancers that I've taught in a conservatory school; dancers from beginning levels to adults in my own studio; these strategies work on students with no dance experience in community settings; and, on professional dancers that I taught regularly in Florida and Arizona as well as all levels of university dancers. These strategies have been successful for different body types and different dance genres. That's why I believe these strategies will help you write your story!

INTRODUCING THE SPINE STRATEGIES

The SPINE strategies are a set of five personal approaches to the "how" of movement. The SPINE addresses movement technique from the perspective of the mover. The five personal strategies are: stretch roads, pressing flair, interpreting, neutralizing joint points, and economizing. Each strategy encompasses one aspect of movement:

S – *stretch roads* will give you a personalized interior mapping system of your moving. Most often stretch roads relates to a dynamic alignment of the body allowing you to take risks successfully by staying connected to your body's centers.

P – *pressing flair* will unlock the power of your body's individual architecture. Each body is anatomically distinct; some people have long legs and a short torso- others the reverse; some people have hyperextension; others scoliosis. Whatever makes your body special can be used to help you move with pressing flair. Pressing Flair moves in your body- not an ideal or imagined body.

I – *interpreting* will link your personal technique to artistic options. Linking technique to artistry occurs by alerting you to choices you can make in the moment of movement. Yes, there is a skill to artistry- it's not something you are born with. You can learn to interpret your movements any way you see fit.

N – *neutralizing* joint points will relate the moving joints of your body to each other. When joints are sensed during movement in connection with each other they become a unified whole. You gain control of your movement making your performances more dependable and your abilities more consistent.

E – *economizing* will give you the keys to speed up your movement. Your movement speed can increase because you can be spot specific in the where and the how of movement initiation.

What is innovative about the SPINE strategies is these strategies focus your attention to the *how* of your moving body. These five strategies are ways of knowing your moving body – knowing what your body feels like during movement and knowing where to send energy to accomplish movement goals. You will know "how" to make movement happen from the inside out. With the SPINE strategies you can create whatever movement or fusion of movement styles that you desire. The strategies work across dance genres and can be applied in classical or contemporary ballet techniques, modern styles, contemporary dance fusion, urban, jazz and gymnastics.

Why do you need the SPINE Strategies?

You need the SPINE strategies for four very important reasons: first, the SPINE strategies address current choreographic expectations of 21st century dancers; second, the SPINE strategies are personalized to your body; third, the SPINE strategies use tensegrity as a model for the body as a whole connecting both science and experience of movement; and fourth, the SPINE strategies create healthy movement that can prevent injuries. I now explain each reason more in depth.

The choreographic expectations of 21st century dancers require you to: maneuver your body with an alignment that is dynamic; sense and operate your body as a whole unit; vary the range of your leg rotation from turned in to parallel; initiate movement from many different body parts; blend movements from a variety of dance styles; implement intricate weight changes; balance actively on and off your centers of gravity; manipulate verticality; alter movement tempo quickly without losing form; and, finally, improvise.

These 21st century movement skills require you to move in extreme ways that can best be achieved through experiencing the process of your movement on the way to achieving your movement goals. As a 21st century dancer you are making in the moment adjustments and for that you need to heighten bodily awareness. You need to listen to YOUR body! The SPINE strategies help you to find, define, and use YOUR body!

Dancing in YOUR personal body requires a highly sophisticated awareness of your physicality during movement. That sophistication doesn't come from adopting ideals and making your body conform to those ideals. A sophisticated bodily awareness comes from realizing that yes, your body is like other bodies, but your body is also different and special to you. As a human you have legs, but those legs may be hyperextended, bowed, twisted in the tibia, turned backward or forward in the thigh bone. There is no ideal body, there are only real bodies. And each real body is different and special. Anatomical differences you see, are the norm. The SPINE allows you to personalize these strategies to fit and work in your real body rather than force your body to fit an ideal non-existent imagined body.

Using tensegrity to model the whole body means that from the mover's perspective you are addressing the body as a whole, the way you as a mover experience the body during movement. Tensegrity has a unique history and requires a more detailed explanation that can be found in the glossary.

For now, consider tensegrity as a model that allows you as a mover to conceive of the body moving as a single whole – which is how you sense the body moving. You don't have arms move and everything else take a rest. There is movement but there is also stabilization happening and both are necessary for movement. The body works as a unit, a whole. Understanding tensegrity as a model for the whole body will assist you enormously as you move.

When you start to become more aware of tensegrity you will see that you are sensing what is called complimentary opposites – which is an AND instead of an either/or type of sensation. You sense an up AND a down, a right AND a left, a front AND a back during movement. By sensing both these opposites at once and working with these opposites, you enable yourself to create movement AND support; orientation AND stabilization, as you move.

Working with tensegrity also means that you will find there is not just one center of the body but two. The two centers or bodily hubs as I call them, are located in the sacrum and in the scapulae or shoulder blades. These are the areas where the limbs (arms and legs) connect to the physical spine and these areas require increased attention and connection for you to remain stable and supported during the constant weight changes that is called dance.

Healthy movement means that injuries are prevented. Throughout this book I detail important scientific studies and ideas that support how each of the SPINE strategies create healthy movement. I initially experienced how the SPINE strategies create healthy movement because as a professional ballerina I did not have any major injury, no surgeries, no knee replacements, no arthroscopies, no dislocated shoulders, etc. In using these SPINE strategies and dancing in a wide variety of dance genres for ten years I managed to stay injury free. Since teaching these SPINE strategies I am often overwhelmed by the amount of students who tell me their knees no longer ache in outward rotation, their ankles strengthen, and their clicking hips stop clicking.

It is my belief the SPINE strategies create healthy movement because these strategies situate an individual dancer in her own body. Then the strategies use all the special differences of that body to excel in movement. I believe that by actually using what makes one's body special, one can surpass the limits of one's body with the SPINE strategies and create healthy movement.

How can this Book help you?

This book will increase self, or *somatic*, awareness of your body during movement and it will accomplish that feat by providing you with information that focuses your dancing practice onto you and your body. Most of the dancers I've encountered know very well the way they need to look, the issue is always how to make that happen with her/his body. So to take the focus off of what you need to look like doesn't mean that your knowledge of what you need to look like goes away. What happens is you find ways to allow that movement goal to happen instead of forcing the goal to happen. There are many ways to accomplish this change in you: you pay more attention to the process of your movement and less to the goal of your movement; you allow yourself to experiment and explore instead of dictate to yourself; you allow your movement to come from your body instead of trying to match an ideal body.

The one example I give to students who look at me quizzically when I explain somatic awareness is this: let's say you are going to drive from Phoenix to Los Angeles. To accomplish the goal you just get on the Interstate 10 and keep going. But it would be ludicrous to get onto the expressway and not take any notice of the cars that butt in front of you, the changes in speed or lanes or the sounds your car makes as you drive. At this point in time you can't just get into a car and onto the road and that's it! You have to pay attention to the process of you driving all the time or you crash! The same is true when you dance. You have to pay attention to the process of what your body feels like as you move in order to create your movement goal of a turn, or an inversion, etc.

Attending to the process of your movement can also be helped enormously by not relying on the visual. Usually dancers rely on seeing themselves more to check the move; or on seeing someone else move to know how to do the move. But continual visual checking as you are moving takes you out of the process and focuses your attention on goals. Thus, to help you disrupt your habits of relying on the visual I have not provided you with any pictures or illustrations in this book.

I have thought long and hard about this and I chose no illustrations for this book so that you would break the traditional patterns of you seeing what is necessary and then replicating that. You need to experiment for yourself and find your way to do what I ask of you in this book. If you continue to seek information outside yourself by looking at pictures or matching your body to the shape of another's you are relying on outside information that will allow you to shut down what you are experiencing in YOUR body.

You need to start from YOUR body not someone else's. Therefore there are no pictures. If you desperately need to see something video *yourself*! That is the best way. Watch yourself move and you will see if what you are experiencing creates the movement goal that you need. You may not believe that taking away the visual and focusing on experimentation and exploration of the process of one's movement can achieve the results that are necessary, so here are some testimonials from my students. Here is what one student wrote about that journey for her:

For so many years I was always concentrating on the big pictures instead of the pathway that one must go through to reach these high goals. I tried to achieve complex movements such as beaten allegro steps and multiple turns without first correcting the flaws in my basic technique. Instead of going through the process and finding all of the intricate details in my body, I would always set myself up for failure by reaching for an unattainable goal. This class has taught me how not to think in such a way. Through taking the warm-up slowly, observing other students, and adding more difficult concepts little by little each week, I now understand that this process-oriented approach is what will make me a successful dancer. Never have I achieved so much in my technique in such a short period of time, and I am positive that this is due to process-oriented movement. Through using the SPINE technique I can notice the changes in my body from day to day, and these changes no longer throw my movement off. By sensing my stretch roads and being aware of concepts such as pressing flair and neutralizing joint points, I can work from the inside of my body instead of just trying to imitate the dancers around me. I have learned that every dancer feels movement differently, and I must listen to what my body is telling me instead of comparing my technique to everyone else.

Another dancer's story:

I definitely see a difference between working with a goal-oriented thought pattern and working with a process-oriented pattern. In a process- oriented thought pattern, the dancer is not thinking so much about how high the leg is kicking or how many rotations you are making. The thought process has switched and is focusing on what tools are needed in order to complete the movement. These tools are things like tapping into your stretch roads and using the idea of pressing flair. The dancer is making a mental note of where his or her body is on that particular day and then making the adjustments for that day. This way of thinking does not allow the dancer to have a certain thought process or regiment for a particular move since this body can vary from day to day. Instead the dancer develops a mental inventory of the body and then can take that information and make the proper adjustments. All of these ideas are designed to just help you tap into you.

These two students are the norm and not the exceptions. So in answer to how can this book help you I would say this book can help you to find a way to enhance your experience of movement through weaning you away from tunnel vision focus on the goals and widening your awareness to the process of your movement. This book can help you by lessening your need to see the movement and increase your ability to feel the movement as you work to match what you feel to how your body looks.

HOW TO USE THIS BOOK

You can start with whatever strategy you feel you need most, but my suggestion would be to begin in this order.

First, with **stretch roads** as this strategy is the simplest one to find in your body and the most important in terms of creating a healthy dynamic posturing for yourself.

Second, I would invite you to work on **pressing flair** as this strategy is the one many of my students have found gives them whole body awareness most rapidly.

Third, I would recommend **neutralizing joint points**. This strategy addresses the body in relationship to itself and informs you how best to utilize turnout as a means of controlling movement.

After you have a sense of these three strategies and how they work together then proceed to **interpreting** to see how you can color and highlight your movement.

Lastly, **economizing** will give you the speed you need to perform contemporary choreography and help you to distill your movement effort into highly efficient sensations.

This order of stretch roads, pressing flair, neutralizing joint points, interpreting and economizing is the order in which I teach students when I teach **SPINE** strategies in the studio. (It is also the order of my workbook *Using SPINE Strategies* that accompanies this book should you wish a week-by-week plan with many exercises and suggestions for how to work with the strategies).

The structure of the chapters in this book are also important. I have started each chapter with a warm up section where I alert you to the language I've chosen to name each of the SPINE strategies. I chose simple names for the strategies that would be packed with information about the qualities that a particular strategy gives you in movement. Thus, the names of each strategy are an attempt to communicate simply to you what you sense as you do that strategy.

Each chapter has an explanation of the strategy and how best to use it, and this will differ with each strategy as each strategy requires something different.

Following is a section called: Herstory where I detail the history of how each strategy came into being. Providing you with this type of intellectual archeology of how ideas were formed by me as a dancer and developed for you as a dancer is innovative. You as a dancer get to look into how another dancer put the pieces together. So, in the hopes that more dancers will begin to articulate how and why a personal understanding of movement developed I provide you with this information and then show you how my story may awaken in you that particular SPINE strategy.

Since all strategies are truly integrated during movement each chapter contains a short explanation of how that particular strategy integrates with the others. Sometimes you might discover this integration on your own while working on a specific strategy or you might want to use these ideas for further exploration to find an integration.

There is also a section on how each SPINE strategy creates healthy movement. In this section I connect the SPINE strategies to formal research on the moving body so you can see possible health benefits from these strategies.

Lastly, in each chapter are ways to implement that particular strategy NOW! While I advocate patience when working on the SPINE strategies, I also know that sometimes you need to improve immediately in some manner and so each chapter contains suggestions for how you can sense the strategy now.

I explain difficult or unfamiliar terms throughout the book, but I also wanted you to have more in-depth information so at the end of the five chapters is a glossary of terms that I use throughout the book and also ways to further your understanding on these ideas. I strongly suggest that you use this section to enhance your understanding of all terminology used.

STRETCH ROADS

Warm-up to Stretch Roads

This warm-up to the stretch roads prepares you to use the stretch roads strategy by understanding how the choice of the words stretch and roads connects to the sensation of this strategy during movement.

The word stretch clues you to the elastic quality of the sensation you feel using this strategy. Elastic indicates a give and take type of stretch. As you experiment with the quality of stretch in your movement, work to sense a morning yawn type of stretch instead of a pull your body apart type of sensation.

Road reminds you of something moving in two different directions. The road in Stretch Roads helps you to draw lines of energy emanating from your limbs through your torso and in the opposite direction somewhere in the body. Roads helps you sense the two way direction as well as the give AND take of the stretch in your body. Sensing this two way connection means that you key into the tensegrity of your body by sensing complimentary opposites (right AND left, up AND down, front AND back) during movement.

Your limbs are the beginnings and transitions of the roads to connect you with the space around you. At first you may just sense one arm or one leg and you may only sense the stretch going away from your body. That's fine at first. But don't stop there. Allow the roads to go in two directions. Let the stretch along the road become an organic movement that has flow and direction.

Stretch Roads Strategy and Purpose

Strategy: Stretch roads creates and monitors the energy pathways of complimentary opposites during movement.

Purpose: Stretch roads mentally draws an interior mapping system that gives you control and keeps you connected to the two bodily centers as you dynamically align yourself through the flow of creating, maintaining, and transitioning shapes.

Understanding and using the stretch roads strategy for the purpose of drawing an interior mapping system connects your body and its movements to the space around you. The result is you might start imagining your body creating, sustaining, and transitioning geometric lines of energy as you move. The flow of these mental images connects to an alignment of the body that is dynamic allowing for what I call the cycle of stretch roads.

The Cycle of Stretch Roads

Consider that the process of dancing means you create shapes, sustain shapes and then transition into other shapes. This never-ending cycle of creating sustaining, and transitioning bodily shapes needs to be regulated and monitored. How? Through bodily negotiation of lines of energy by the dancer control in movement is manifested. That's the purpose of stretch roads – control during shape changes.

Using stretch roads you gain the ability to sense, monitor and anticipate the movements of your limbs and torso making bodily shapes as you create, sustain and transition these shapes by sensing the elastic stretch of your limbs through your torso and into the space around you.

With stretch roads you can go through the cycle of creating, sustaining and transitioning positions all the while maintaining support for your limbs in the torso because stretch roads helps you to connect the limbs to the two centers in your body (the scapular hub and the sacral hub- see glossary for more info). You maintain balance and demonstrate an alignment that is dynamic and able to handle the ever-changing positions of dance.

Cycle of Stretch Roads: Using Stretch Roads to Create a Shape

To understand the cycle of stretch roads start with a simple position: Stand on two feet with both arms outstretched to the side. In this position feel the stretch as a gentle elastic yawn expanding your energy through your arms into space and through your legs into the ground. By energy I mean a sense of length and a sense of direction for the stretch. Increase this sense of stretch so much that all you sense is stretching outwards. Understand that with this type of stretch you have gone past an important sensed marker for yourself. Pull back, discover how to be more elastic. Sense elasticity in the stretch almost as if you sense energy flowing back into your torso from your fingertips and your feet back into your torso at the same time as you sense stretching outwards. Or you might sense your right AND left arms in a single line of energy flow outwards – you are sensing a complimentary opposite if you can feel both arms connected. And you are sensing a bit of how to maintain a position.

Cycle of Stretch Roads: Using Stretch Roads to Maintain a Shape

Experiment with this same position to maintain it. You are on two legs so it's not difficult but work to sense the subtleties of the energy flow in your body through the stretch roads. A lot of times students are doing it but don't realize it because they expect a huge sensation. The sensing of your energy is more like a whisper than a shout. Listen for the whisper. Sense your right arm extended to the side, where then is the opposite stretch – the left stretch? Can you connect the right arm stretch through your torso to the left arm stretch? Can you sense this stretch as a single stretch road? Good.

Now what about the rest of your limbs, i.e., the legs? Can you sense the left leg? Where is that stretch? Down into the floor? Okay, now where is there an up stretch in the exact opposite direction? For me, it's in the back of the head that stretches up towards the ceiling.

What then about the right leg? Can you sense a down stretch? Okay. Now connect the left leg and right leg with the head finding a way to sense an entire stretch road going both up and down at the same time. Now connect that up and down stretch with the side-to-side stretch going on in the right and left arms.

Sensing all these stretch roads simultaneously is the ability of stretch roads to create a mapping system sort of like a GPS of your body as you move. You are using the sensation of the complimentary opposites that travel along your stretch roads to know where your body is in space.

Cycle of Stretch Roads: Using Stretch Roads to Transition a Shape

Now you want to transition from this position to another position. Transitions require you to sense a full extension of all stretch roads through all limbs without pulling yourself apart before you change the position. Choose where to initiate the next position by continuing to stretch through your four limbs. Let's say you are going to a turned in passé with both arms overhead thus you will need to transfer all your weight to the left leg as well. So going back to the standing position you sense two stretch roads in this position the one going up and down through the head and two legs and the one going side to side through the right and left arms. Now to transition to standing on the left leg with the right leg going into a turned in passé position at the knee and both arms coming overhead here are the stretch roads in action:

Sense the stretch road going down in the right and left leg against the upwards sensation of the head AND the left and right stretch through the body and into the left and right arms.

Continue stretching the left leg down and connect that stretch sensation through to the up in the head – release the right leg from this stretch road.

At this point you are going to move the right leg into the turned in passé so put a bit more sensation of length into the arms sensing the right and left stretch road.

Move the right leg into the turned in passé as you sense the morphing of the left and right stretch roads in the arms. You will then sense ever so much stronger the up and down stretch through the left leg and out the back of the head stretching up. The side to side stretch road is then taken up by the elbows with the right elbow stretching to the right and the left elbow stretching to the left without destroying the circle that is 5th position.

Start Exploring Stretch Roads by Questioning Yourself

Now it's your turn to explore the stretch roads for yourself. Start by questioning yourself as you create your positions to find where the stretch roads travel through your body. Very simply the stretch roads strategy is about control and stability as you extend your limbs into space. I include the head and sometimes the tail as limbs depending on your position. So you have at least four limbs (two arms, two legs) and sometimes five (two arms, two legs and the head) and sometimes six (two arms, two legs, a head and a tail). It will be through these limbs that you need to sense the stretch roads. Start with questioning yourself as you move to find where all these limbs are. Listen for your body's whispered response.

Questioning myself was how I mapped my first stretch road and discovered this strategy for myself. I started by saying to myself, okay, I have my left arm in front creating an energy going forward now where in my body is the energy that is going back? I then identified it was through my right arm that energy was going back. I kept questioning myself during adagios, allegros, in the warm-up hunting for these oppositional energies. I either found them or created them if I didn't sense them.

I began to find more and more quickly where the energy going in the opposite direction was and then I started to ask myself: can I sense the entire length of this energy rather than dividing the energy into two separate sensations of front and back? I would ask myself where does that line of energy go through my torso? From what body part to what body part am I sensing a tensional relationship? Without knowing it I was sensing complimentary opposites in my movement.

Sensing a complimentary opposite in the body means that opposite directions of energy exist together instead of one direction overruling and making the other opposite direction disappear. Sensing complimentary opposites during movement means you sense the tensegrity of your body in action. The tensegrity in your movement means that your body knows how already to make shapes by sensing left and right, up and down, front and back. That's how your body moves and counterbalances itself to keep your body from falling. The point with sensing and using the complimentary opposites of stretch roads is to key into how your body moves rather than imposing an artificial approach on your body.

Herstory of Stretch Roads

Here is the history of the ideas, teachers, and practices that formed for me the strategy of stretch roads that I am presenting to you in this book.

The seeds of the stretch roads strategy were planted when I was a trainee at Harkness House in the 1970s. There I learned I had hyperextended legs and that my entire neuro-muscular patterning for turnout was incorrect. My pelvis was the key to fixing the problem according to Maria Vegh, assistant director of Harkness. She said make the thigh joint on the supporting leg flat and imagine both hips were above the barre. I kept these ideas alive in my body for an entire class even though I had trouble breathing (which I now know means that I was engaging the transverse abdominis and that sensing breathing difficulty is normal; it went away the stronger my transverse abdominis got). Engaging the transverse abdominis was the first step towards sensing a stretch road.

Then Anne Hebard, also at Harkness, suggested I break traditional ballet rules and bend my working knee on a battement tendu as it came in to fifth position. The request was so that I didn't push back into my hyperextended knees. As I bent my knee I began to sense a heel to inner thigh connection on the working leg as my leg went in and out of fifth position. This connection felt like there was a taut string attaching the heel to the top inside of the working leg. I could feel nothing coming from the quadriceps or lateral aspect of my working leg. These new sensations of heel and inner thigh became my modus operandi for taking my leg in and out of fifth. The heel to inner thigh connection was for me the second step towards creating a stretch road.

Fast forward to Chicago Ballet. A guest teacher in the company morning class said to contact the pyramidalis muscle (a small triangular muscle attached from the pubic crest to just under the navel that when engaged stops you from urinating mid-stream). Engagement of the pyramidalis I now believe, allowed my body to create a lengthening of the supporting muscles in the torso. I found how to engage my quadratus lumborum (a muscle that connects the ribs to the pelvis) to find the height in my body that everyone tells you about when they say "lift up." I began to have the ability to direct where my energy went in the lower half of my body. I sensed kinesthetically that I was smaller when I engaged these core muscles in my torso, yet I looked to others lifted and taller. Engaging the pyramidalis, sensing yourself as small but looking to someone else as taller is the third step.

Then it was Eugene Tanner, ballet master of Chicago Ballet, who said to contract together the fronts of my armpits (my pectorals). What??? I searched anatomy books to understand what he was talking about and why pectorals might assist in any upper arm connections. I discovered a neurological connection of the third finger directly to the sixth and seventh cervical vertebrae. I wiggled my third finger and sensed a very, very, very subtle sensation underneath the upper arm between the elbow and shoulder.

Then it hit me, the heel to sitz bone (inner thigh, pyramidalis) connection that helps the dancer to connect to the torso and center (sacral hub) is equivalent to the third finger to underarm and pectoral connection linking the arm to the torso via the scapula to the physical spine which is the physical center of the body. It was HUGE when I realized that the ideas used for the legs could be applied to the arms. Legs = Arms is part four.

Next, a bit of Eastern philosophy mixed with body mechanics. In the martial arts one sends the internal energy of the body beyond the physical limits of the body. So, okay, I reasoned if I had a hip problem, I could best fix the hip if I thought of what controlled that hip and not go crazy thinking of just the hip itself like it was inside a box. I had to think outside of the physical box of my problem. This out of the physical box realization was the key to me finding how to put all these parts together for the stretch roads theory.

Putting all these steps together for the stretch roads strategy spanned years of trial and error. But when I did it I had a controllable and supported alignment that was dynamic because I created stretch roads where I could sense complimentary opposites as I extended my body into space.

Applying Herstory to You

Here are ways you might apply my journey to yours:

To create a position find the complimentary opposites – question yourself

To sustain a position engage all the complimentary opposites – sensed all together in the body

To transition a position into another select which stretch roads to maintain as you initiate the movement to the next position where you begin once again to question yourself to find the complimentary opposites

STRETCH ROADS AND HEALTHY MOVEMENT

In this section I provide for you connections to kinesiological research that demonstrate how and why Stretch Roads as a strategy works to keep your body healthy during movement.

Attend to Your Process to Prevent Problems

Stretch roads produces healthy movement by making you attend to the process of your movement. You know your goal, what you can't be sure of is how you are going to accomplish it. And what you need is a way to fix problems as they pop up. Staying aware of your stretch roads helps you to anticipate these problems; you lessen the time between a stimulus telling you something needs adjustment (like you're falling too much to the right) and your response to fix it.

Using stretch roads doesn't mean you dance without errors or problems, but that you can fix them in the moment of movement so you appear that you are dancing without issues.

You can also prevent injuries such as pulls, strains or even more severe traumatic ones by making the slight adjustments in your alignment that stretch roads makes you aware of.

For more information on process and goal, stimulus and response, read Steven Chatfield and Sherrie Barr's article *Towards a Testable Hypothesis of Training Principles for the Neuromuscular Facilitation of Human Movement* in the *Dance Research Journal* Spring of 1994.

Sense Length

Keeping a sense of length in your body before and as you move gives you more physical power during movement. A muscle has the strongest contraction after it has been stretched to length. Thus, the plié where the gastrocnemius muscle (calf) stretches prior to extending the leg gives the ability to jump higher because the gastrocnemius after being stretched to length contracts with greater force. This same principle of lengthening before you contract a muscle works for other muscles as well.

Sensing length by using stretch roads connects to healthy movement because when you sense length you work your muscles efficiently and this keeps you from muscle strain, over-recruitment and gripping. It's the muscular imbalances that lead all dancers and all bodies really down the road towards problems. Muscular imbalances affect the integrity of the joints and can lead ultimately over a long period of misuse (decades) to osteoarthritis.

The main point here is that the more you can work your muscles efficiently the more the body can maintain a good tensional integrity (tensegrity) in your muscle tissue and the less chance you have of injury due either to some misstep where the muscle tissue tears or to osteoarthritis later in life after muscular imbalances have disrupted joint integrity.

Googling stretch reflex or myotactic reflex will give you a more detailed explanation of how contracting a muscle prior to using it gives it more power and makes it more efficient.

Rely on Your Reflexes

With stretch roads you tap into your body's reflexes – both righting reflexes to help you balance/counterbalance and propriospinal reflexes to help finding cross-lateral stability to support gesture leg movements.

Together, relying on these reflexes allows your body to organize your bodily positions using counterbalance. You can also challenge the vertical more often by going farther off-balance knowing that the reflexes will monitor your position from vertical to off-balance and back to vertical.

When you are not taking risks with your positions perhaps it's because you are shutting down the torso. That means you are working against your own physical needs of counterbalancing to achieve balance. With a shut-down torso you are encouraging muscles to grip and over recruiting muscles to support your torso that don't compensate for your position with counterbalance: gripping is never an injury prevention approach.

Kinesiological evidence states the torso must adjust, and compensate for your legs moving. One study of a *grand battement devant* done by Rhonda Rhyman and Donald Ranney found that the pelvis and spine are directly involved and compensate when the leg kicks to the front. The study shows that the physicality of the *grand battement*, i.e., what you actually need to experience does not match traditional ballet aesthetics of a torso not moving when the leg kicks to the front.

As a professional ballerina my torso moved a lot. I used stretch roads and moved my torso yet it looked as though my torso wasn't moving. That's the key! To move and yet look as if you didn't move. How?

Connect your limbs to the bodily central hubs using stretch roads and then listen to your body for the signs of the reflex through sensing counterbalance.

Allow your reflexes to work.

How did I make this work in a *grand battement devant*? I sensed the connection to my lower bodily center before the tendu by using pressing flair to sense both my kicking leg and the leg about to release from the floor to find my stretch roads. My reflexes allowed me to kick high as long as I maintained connection to the stretch road on my supporting leg and the stretch roads going through my arms. By sensing these connections I would control the risks I took.

You can find the Rhyman and Ranney research in the *Dance Research Journal* Volume 11 1978-1979. The article is entitled: *A Preliminary Investigation of Two Variations of the "Grand Battement Devant."*

For more about reflexes the Sally Fitt book *Dance Kinesiology* has information as well as just googling righting reflex or propriospinal reflex.

3 Ways to Start Implementing Stretch Roads NOW!

S-l-o-w Down

Work on slow movements in adagios or maybe just two steps in a slow combination. With the slower tempo you can take the time to question yourself and find your complimentary opposites. Discover part of the road and then through questioning add on the rest of the road. Step by step.

Take a Breath

Breathing is essential to you being able to sense your body. Once you hold your breath you disable the ability to sense the complimentary opposites. No breathing means you just grip and hold. So take a breath!

Shhhh! Listen for the Whisper

Your body shouts only when it's in pain. The rest of the time your body speaks to you in whispers. Sensing your energy in movement along with the good tensional relationships between your muscles, i.e., the tugs and pulls, that is the language of your body speaking to you. Too much forcing, gripping, or dictating to your body can silence your body's voice. So listen for the whisper of the elastic stretch of stretch roads as you extend your limbs into space.

Integrating Stretch Roads with Other SPINE Strategies

Pressing Flair: Press into the floor or air to initiate movement and then follow through morphing the press into sensing your stretch roads. This morphing recycles your energy and controls your moves.

Interpreting: Use stretch roads to add flourish and sustain moves.

Neutralizing Joint Points: Keep aware of your energy when extending a flexed limb by using stretch roads.

Economizing: Sense the fully extended limb keeping limb-torso connections with stretch roads to move quickly.

PRESSING FLAIR

Warm-up to Pressing Flair

In this warm up to pressing flair, the second SPINE strategy, the two words pressing and flair give you important information about what to do and where to do it. The what to do is pressing; the where to do it is the floor and the air.

The word pressing suggests an action where you sense a steady pressure. It's the idea of a steady dynamic that's important because you want to listen as you press for what I call the tensegretic response; this is where parts of the body that can support the parts that are pressing respond to your steady pressure by creating a tensional connection to where you are pressing. Pressing and then sensing the tensegretic response tells you that whatever you are doing will be connected to the central hubs of your body.

Flair is a combined word (floor + air). I invite you to consider the floor and air as your partners as you move. Count on them. Press into them and your body will create the tensegretic response that will sustain you.

Pressing Flair Strategy and Purpose

Strategy: Pressing flair is applying steady pressure to the floor and air during movement.
Purpose: Pressing flair unlocks the power of the architecture of your body to support you through eliciting the tensegretic response.

Some of my students believe pressing flair is the most important SPINE strategy. These students have told me that it was through pressing flair that they found connections to the other strategies and ultimately a sense of the whole body moving. I believe pressing flair is so important to my students because it assists them in connecting all limbs to the physical spine during movement!!!

Here are the muscular connections that I have found are activated when using pressing flair. These chain of connections unites you from the tip of your limb to your physical spine:

When pressing the arms into the air (or the floor if you are doing some movement inverted) here are the sensed set of connections:

Fingertips (third finger specifically) connected to the flexor carpi ulnaris (muscle in your forearm)
Flexor carpi ulnaris connected to the triceps;
Triceps connected to the scapula;
Scapula connected to the rhomboids;
Rhomboids connected to the physical spine

When pressing the legs into the floor or air this chain of connections is activated:

Heel connected to the pyramidalis (pelvic floor, inner thigh);
Pyramidalis connected to the transverse abdominis (inner corset);
Transverse abdominis connected from the pelvis to the ribs and physical spine

From these sets of sensed muscular connections (sometimes called a kinetic chain) you connect movement to the physical spine in your body. Through the physical spine connection you are also connecting the shoulder girdle to the pelvic girdle. The end result is that all four limbs (arms and legs) are in communication with each other via the physical spine. Pretty cool!

Herstory of Pressing Flair

The first element of what came to be the pressing flair concept that I realized as a dancer was the physical importance of the plié. I cannot fully recollect when my body began to use the plié to full capacity nor can I attribute an understanding of how to work the plié to a specific teacher's feedback, although I know many teachers and directors discussed the *plié*. For me, images of other dancers helped enormously, especially watching Rudolph Nureyev who I distinctly remember impressed me with his *plié*. I watched fascinated the opening film scene at the barre in *I am a Dancer* where Nureyev pushes, and I mean really pushes his foot into the floor staying in *demi-plié* as his leg goes out in a *battement tendu*. I experimented to get the feel of staying in *plié* a little longer and sensed enormous power in my body from the ground up.

Peeling my foot off the floor by pressing, I attribute to Elizabeth Carroll, at Harkness, who would come into class and teach us ballet technique in her pointe shoes. Everyone in class was mesmerized watching her feet undulate as if they were going through the floor in barre exercises.

The upper body resistance of pressing flair grew out of my work with Eugene Tanner, ballet master of Chicago Ballet. When I began to understand the body structure more, I realized that the same pectoral pressure that assisted me in finding the upper body in the stretch roads could also be the reason I was able to press into the air with my arms. What I didn't realize at the time was that I was connecting into the bodily center of the scapulae in the upper body. Later, when instructing at Southern Ballet Theatre in Orlando how to work the body as a unit, I used the word flair as a compound for floor and air, the two surfaces the dancer approaches with pressing to help dancers remember the arms and legs press into the environment together.

It took quite a bit of time to understand that the paradox of buoyancy and weight I feel in my body when I use pressing flair are both elements of a tensegretic structure in motion. Pressing flair elicits a tensegretic response that connects you to the physical spine – the center of your body.

Pressing Flair and Healthy Movement

Protect Your Knees

When you are in a *plié*, pressing against the floor on the ascent connects you more to the hamstrings than the quadriceps. Instead of pulling yourself up with your quadriceps from the bottom of any *plié* you are ascending by pressing against the floor and using your hamstrings to extend your legs. When you press into the floor and connect to the hamstrings on the ascent you feel as if you are floating up from the base of the *plié* all the while sensing a groundedness through the legs to and through the floor. Connecting to the hamstrings (the back of the legs) is important for the health of your knees.

Karen Clippinger-Robertson did a study in 1985 on the *plié* in second position in ballet. She found dancers who engaged their hamstrings when ascending from the *plié* had far less injury to the knees than those who straightened the legs using the quadriceps (tops of the legs). The *plié*, she concluded, was not bad for you. Rather it was how you came up from the bottom of the *plié* that was the issue.

Karen Clippinger-Robertson's article appeared in the 1985 issue of *Kinesiology for Dance* and is entitled *Mechanical and Anatomical Factors Relating to the Incidence and Etiology of Patellofemoral Pain in Dancers.*

Prevent Patellofemoral Syndrome

Patellofemoral syndrome is where the tracking of the kneecap (patella) pulls to the side rather than staying straight up and down when your knees bend. The reason the kneecap goes to the side is because there is too much pull from the side of the leg. While too much pull from the side of the leg can occur for a variety of structural reasons, there is also a strong possibility that a muscular imbalance is the reason for the sideways pull.

Dancers can create this syndrome through sending the kinetic chain of energy to the outside of the leg rather than to the inside during movement. Not connecting from the heel to the pyramidalis during movement can, over time, contribute to a tight iliotibial band (on the side of the thigh) leading to a muscular imbalance with the outside of the leg being stronger than the inside.

Over pointing the foot and thus accessing the outside of the leg rather than the inside is another way to create the muscular imbalances that contribute to this syndrome. Think of pointing your heel and then just extending that point with your toes to prevent over pointing.

Lastly, pulling yourself up from the bottom of pliés can also create the imbalance in patellar tracking by engaging the quadriceps. Use pressing flair to push down into the floor to extend the legs.

For more information on patellofemoral syndrome I suggest you google the term to find both websites with more info and YouTube videos.

Work With Your Body

By staying connected to your bodily centers you stand a better chance of preventing injury because you are working WITH your body. Your body has built in reflexes that can take care of movement for you rather than you dictating to your body what the goal of a movement is.

Working with your body means allowing those reflexes to alert you when necessary adjustments or movements need to be made. Righting reflexes help keep your balance and prevent falling. Propriospinal reflexes are involved in creating natural opposition. The crossed-extensor reflex helps you to turn around your natural axis.

Reflexes are great things to have working for you because the reflex signal only goes to the spinal cord and then comes back to the muscles. Reflexes do not have to be processed consciously in the brain. Reflexes are part of your bodily intelligence. That's how you can misstep causing your ankle to twist climbing mountains and in lightning speed your ankle comes right back without injury. Reflexes operate at warp speed in your body.

Pressing flair connects you into this warp speed so you know how far is far enough when moving. Pressing flair connects you to your bodily centers and together with the reflexes can make nanosecond adjustments that can save you from injury. You want to use strategies that assist you in working with your body.

The idea of working with your body comes from exploring your body somatically through experimentation and discovery. Check out more information online about your reflexes if you wish more detailed or technical explanations.

5 Ways to Implement Pressing Flair NOW!

Begin with the Bends

In terms of dance movement I would start to find pressing flair in a *plié*, a simple bending of the knees. Try this partnered experiment to feel what happens in a *plié*. Have your partner stand behind you and put their hands on your shoulders. Do a plié in any position - just a *demi-plié* is fine. When you are about to ascend have your partner press down on your shoulders – heavy enough for you to have to work to ascend, but light enough that you can move without over gripping. Working against that pressure from your shoulders you only have one option and that is to press into the floor with your metatarsals/midfoot to come up. You will sense the metatarsal/midfoot connection to your hamstrings. You will sense buoyancy and groundedness simultaneously. It will feel like you are coming up from underwater to the surface. That's pressing flair in action!

Solo the Arms

Experiment with moving ONLY your arms in a combination. Keep the legs quiet and do the arms full out - this is the fastest way I know to find out what is going on in your upper body with pressing flair.

Regulate your Air Force

Press with your arms or legs into the air with all the force you can.
Exhausting right? Now press with your arms or legs into the air with no force at all. The point is now you have your limits. Regulate your force somewhere between the limits you just physically sensed and press into the air. Find a good midpoint of force to use when pressing into the air with the arms and legs.

Use All Fours

Getting all four limbs to press simultaneously in any floor/air combination takes a bit of getting used to. It's about co-ordination. Frustration will not help.

Right before you begin to be frustrated go back to working each limb separately. This divide and conquer approach will help you because you are reinforcing the new neuromuscular patterns and increasing your synaptic facilitation of these moves. When you go back to the move, say ten minutes later or next day your body will be better prepared to coordinate all four limbs. With co-ordination comes whole body integration.

Weight a While

Everyone's upper body is unique. Yours may be strong in some areas and weak in others. Google the muscles in the back, find out what ones of yours are weak and weight condition to gain strength in your upper back. The upper back is traditionally weak and often tight in dancers, but you can take action to strengthen and stretch your upper back. Do your shoulders droop forwards when you relax? Do push-ups! Is your upper back tight? Use a tennis ball/ foam roller or check out YouTube for stretching exercises for the upper back. Stretch to make your muscles useful to you. Strengthen them to prevent injury. Either way you will be creating more readiness in your upper back to press your arms into the air.

Integrating Pressing Flair with other SPINE strategies

Stretch roads: Press to transition from fully extended shapes. You will keep body length and stay balanced as you continue to move.
Interpreting: Adjust the dynamic of pressing and make your personal viewpoint manifest in your movement.
Neutralizing Joint Points: Press to achieve initial kinetic impetus to change shapes without losing control.
Economizing: Initiate from distal body points by pressing with a light touch into the air. You will need less pressing than you anticipate to achieve speed.

INTERPRETING

Warm-up to Interpreting

Before you begin to work on the third SPINE strategy of interpreting my choice of the word interpreting was to provide a way to understand the physical process of what is actually going on when the dancer adds that extra layer of personal emotion, charisma. Maybe you call it performance skills? Artistry? These different names all have one thing in common they all mean you as a dancer are interpreting the moves you are making with your body. When you interpret you put your individuality into the movement, your view, your emotions, your flavor. And there is a physical technique to adding this interpretive layer.

Interpreting Strategy and Purpose

Strategy: Interpreting is the dancer constructing individuality in movement by directing personal perceptions during movement.

Purpose: Interpreting will link your personal skill level of technique to your artistic choices to add that extra layer of performance to your movement.

Interpreting, the third SPINE strategy, is a way to train the skill of choice into the dancer. Using interpreting you choose to open your personal perception and attention to your sense of what is available to you in that moment of movement.

Interpreting empowers you because you are made aware of the options you have at THAT moment! You choose. With interpreting you take responsibility for how you write your moves in space.

Refining the skill of choice is different from making sure that you follow directions or look the same as the person next to you. Dance training often gives the impression that you don't have options you just have to achieve your movement goal, but rest assured you have plenty of options. To find them you must engage yourself with the moment and the environment.

Interpreting is an action word. It means that you have to do something – interpreting doesn't just happen! Interpreting is a way to negotiate with the context that surrounds you. And you negotiate by choosing and then attending to that choice.

What is most important about including interpreting as a strategy in the technique training classroom and in the philosophy of technique for movement is that up until now this type of concern was left to rushed rehearsals or completely forgotten in the midst of a technique class. Interpreting was considered as something special and not available to everyone. But interpreting skills are available to everyone. Some dancers may be better at interpreting than others, but the skills to interpret are available and can be trained in the technique classroom. The issue to realize is that interpreting is a technique, a skill, a way to choose how you move your body.

Where to start?

When you interpret movement the skill is in what you are paying attention to. Understanding what you are paying attention to comes from learning more about how your perception works. What you choose to perceive contributes to why and how you are paying attention to your body as you move. Start with understanding the three perceptual pathways that are available to you in perceiving your body.

Interoception

Interoception is the first perceptual pathway. A perceptual pathway means that in the nervous system there are pathways taking information to and from your brain. I think of these pathways like highways. Along these highways information is transferred to the brain on certain aspects of reality. In the interoceptive pathway information continues to your brain on a second by second basis about your heart rate, your breathing, your body temperature, and any pain you might be experiencing. Your body's sensors, which are special nerve cells, relay this information to your brain to maintain your health. For the most part information on heart rate, breathing, temperature and even possible pain are all in the background of your attention. This information doesn't come to your conscious attention unless there is a change that warrants your attention. If you are in pain anywhere in your body, if your heart starts to beat too quickly, if you start to gasp for air the interoceptive pathway brings this information to your conscious attention so you can do something about it. As a dancer most often you will pay attention to the information the interoceptive pathway is sending you when you work on breathing practices and most definitely if you are in pain.

Exteroception

Other dancers, costumes, lights, architecture, sound/music and spatial features and boundaries – these are all examples of information that your exteroceptive pathway brings to your attention. Exteroception is about your nervous system being able to sense what is outside your body so that moving your body can be done without incident.

As a dancer you learn to perceive what is around you for many reasons; so you don't hit anything, so you co-ordinate with other dancers; so you can connect to the music.

Proprioception

The tugs, pulls, tensional relationships your body creates during movement that helps you to sense yourself moving – this is proprioception – the ability of you to sense yourself moving.

As a dancer you work hard to get movement up to a certain level. Part of getting movement to that level is being able to reproduce movement with an outcome that is relatively the same each time you perform that movement. Keying into your proprioception is invaluable to you as a way to sense where your body is and how your body relates to itself to create the shapes and do the moves you are working on.

Now what?

Now that you are aware of the three types of perception how do you use these in interpreting?

You juggle these perceptual pathways constantly as you move. You can be aware of the muscular synergies as you move (proprioception); your breath, heartbeat or pain (interoception); and/or the multitude of items outside your body: other dancers, the instructor, your peers as audience, the architecture, or music (exteroception). You can contract your perception of one area and expand another, synthesize two areas. It's your choice!

You can plan how you want to do the movement, but in the moment of moving all plans dissolve: you find a hole in the floor, your calf suddenly cramps, someone steps on your costume. The technique you need to have is to be able to expand or contract your perception in order to direct your choices as you are moving. Thus, it is important to train for as broad an awareness of your body in the moment of movement as possible.

It's this expanded bodily perceptional awareness used to interpret movement that I've seen time and again dancers have when they learn to juggle interoception, exteroception and proprioception as they move according to circumstances of the situation.

How do you juggle?

You juggle the perceptual pathways by choosing what you pay attention to. The place to start is to find out what exactly you are paying attention to now. I suggest you start by just monitoring what you do pay attention to when you move. Start where you are and then realize that you have choices. You can enhance your attention to one of the perceptual pathways or you can diminish your attention. Here is where no one can tell you what to do. You need to experiment for yourself and see what you find.

What I will suggest however is that you pay attention to the words that you use when you speak to yourself as you move and when you write about your movement. If you find that you are using the word "should" a lot then you know you are keying into the norms, the rules of the dance form you are doing. You are not paying attention to YOUR experience of the movement, but rather paying attention to what someone else told you that you should do. If you find yourself writing phrases like: I sense, I feel, I experience, I attune to, I am aware of – then you know that you are paying attention to YOUR experience of the movement. You know that you are using the SPINE strategies to interpret YOUR moving point of view.

Herstory of Interpreting

Here's how I journeyed to create the interpreting strategy. I was privileged to meet Alicia Alonso, a world renowned prima ballerina assoluta at age thirteen. My studio teacher was Cuca Martinez, Alicia Alonso's sister. In 1970, three of us from Cuca Martinez's studio went to Montreal to watch two weeks of performances of the *Ballet National de Cuba* where this blind prima ballerina took fourteen curtain calls for her interpretation of *Carmen*. At the time I didn't realize how Alonso manipulated her weight through the use of her *plié* or used her heel connection to the rest of her joints to create emotional tension as she extended her leg in a *développé*. All I knew then was how amazing she was and ever since then I have searched for those dancers who could move the audience as Alonso did.

As a professional ballerina just having an appreciation for those that can connect with an audience doesn't help you to know how to do it yourself. So I hunted for connections between technique class exercises and performance artistry. My quest was for why I was learning these specific techniques and how they served me onstage while I was in the midst of moving.

I was in the lighting booth during one of the runs of Ruth Page's *Nutcracker* at Arie Crown Theater in Chicago and the stage manager pointed out how the dancer as the *American Beauty Rose* in Page's *Waltz of the Flowers* would hold an *arabesque* past the allotted time in the music and then quicken up the next few steps. The stage manager said the dancer did this every time she performed, and for him, who saw every one of the twenty-four or so performances, that small intermittent holding of a pose made the piece interesting to watch. I began to experiment with this technique of holding and then quickening my next movements and found this playing with the music proved to be extremely valuable to choosing how to express myself onstage.

My own goal in performing was always to move the audience emotionally. The coaching I received from Larry Long in Chicago came closest to helping me find out how to use the energy in my body expressively. Long would sing the movements for the *Sugar Plum* pas de deux in rehearsal. My partner and I would *arabesque sauté* off to the upstate left corner ready for the diagonal and the pirouettes in the middle of the *pas de deux*. As we would begin the diagonal of lifts and *pirouettes*, Long's voice would be singing at the top of his lungs, "BE-bab-bab-ba-ba-ba (the preparation) YA! (the lift) Ya-zzzzzzzzzzzzzzzz – Yah!" (the *pirouette* finish in *attitude*!). From Long's voice I was clued as to how to attack my movements. His voice guided me to put more energy into this movement or that pose and less in others.

When I began to teach full time, I searched to find an optimal way to instruct dancers in accessing and developing their own performance skills. I now knew myself how to engage the audience, but how to impart this skill to others was a whole other issue. I didn't want to become part of the group of instructors who hold the belief that the more technique you have the more you could do artistically with it – the more you could interpret your moves. I relied on my past experiences of creating sounds in my head and working with the music in the dance technique classroom to assist dancers to interpret, but I knew there was more I could do.

It wasn't until I did my doctorate and investigated embodied perception in dancers that a clear path appeared. I realized it was through perception that I was interpreting movement and that it was during dance technique class that this technique of perceiving myself and my surroundings as I moved was developed.

Applying Herstory to You

Try sounding out your movements. Instead of moving your body invent sounds that represent how you want to interpret the movement. Say those sounds out loud to yourself and then hear yourself saying those sounds as you move. Creating a soundscape of your movement could just knock you out of habits that are keeping you from finding the "I" in interpreting.

Interpreting and Healthy Movement

Don't Erase You

During college when I was studying dance theory I reread my personal journals that I kept during my professional dancing days and found an entry stating that my mood was determined by how the artistic director felt that day. If the director was happy that day when he taught company class, I was happy. If the director was worried, I was worried. And most definitely if the director was in a bad mood, I was in a bad mood. I wrote that my sense of self was erased. I literally wrote the word erased!

I had always worked my body so that it was clay for the director/choreographer to sculpt movement on. It was a hard lesson to learn that being clay doesn't mean erasing yourself.

In teaching interpreting I've found a way to help dancers prevent this self-erasing. I've found that using interpreting in the dance technique class continuously empowers the dancers because I tell the dancers they have a choice as they move and show them possibilities using the interpreting strategy to juggle perceptual pathways. Using interpreting I've found improves a dancer's mental health. I have found no research studies to date that can confirm or disprove my own experiential findings.

Prevent Overtraining

As I understand it placing technique of where the body needs to be above the technique of making choices as you move is a type of overtraining that leads a dancer to stifle the self-impulses during movement. In a word this overtraining for aesthetic techniques can make you hypersensitive to the ideals of your dance form such that you are silencing that all important "I." You deserve to have a view of the movement especially in the moment when you are creating it with your body.

A choreographer's creation does not come into being until your body dances it into view. Your body (re)creates a choreographer's idea. You are physically writing the movement. Thus, without some ability to interpret the movement you are like an echo that has no physical presence. Developing the technique of interpreting movement in your dance technique classroom means that you prevent an imbalance of focus solely on bodily shapes and physical abilities. There are signs and symptoms of overtraining that can be applies to dance training. Google the phrase "dance and overtraining" to find out more.

Find YOUR Physical Limits

Yes, your body has physical limits. Finding these limits can prevent injury. Becoming aware of these limits helps you to define you and is in no way limiting if you choose to capitalize on these limits.

Each body is different. Knowing in an intimate physical way through the use of the SPINE strategies how much you can bend one way, or when you need to press more into the floor, or that you need to focus more on the distal extremities in order to attend to your movement goal is a good thing. This knowledge will assist you in preventing injury because you work WITH and not against your limits. Find your physical limits and exploit them like Bob Fosse (who was pigeon-toed and his technique is turned in) or Marie Taglioni (whose hunched back became the romantic torso position). Many dancers have created entire physical techniques by working with their physical limits. Use Interpreting to find your limits and then use your limits to create a personal technique!

Key into Your Ever-Changing Body

There is now scientific evidence that confirms what many dancers already know – the body changes constantly. As a dancer you are already aware of the every-changing body but how can you allow for change when trying to be dependable and consistent in movement?

By keying into the way you perceive yourself moving (using the strategy of interpreting), you become more able to see your personal patterns of movement. These patterns fluctuate but nonetheless these patterns are important physically for you to investigate in order to dance healthily. By inquiring why your left knee always has problems with a certain move you may find that you are over rotating only on your left side during turns or that you do not include parts of your body when preparing to move the left knee. Keying into your ever-changing body means you are becoming more invested in interpreting your moves.

For more information on bodily changes I suggest you look into the work of Antonio Damasio or Joseph LeDoux to find ways that the body perceives on a second-by-second basis what is happening.

Find and Monitor Your Bodily Responses

Thus, in the most succinct manner what I believe is the purpose of technique class is to provide, you as a dancer with an awareness of your body that serves as the foundation for your experience in performance. The way to do this is to expand your bodily awareness of itself moving, notice more who is dancing around you, and really see and feel the space and time you are dancing in through attending to the music and architecture of the space you are moving in. This approach is using interpreting to attend to your perceptual pathways and ultimately to find and monitor your bodily responses.

Interpreting specifically gives you a workable ability to manipulate your body according to the circumstances of your body at that time on that stage and for that specific performance.

Interpreting is the outgrowth of your ability to sense your moving body in space. The more you sense the more you can manipulate. The more you can manipulate the more choices you have. The more choices you have the more you are in an empowered position to present your body choreographically during the dance event. Choices stem from the space, time and energy of the movement you are doing and the space, time and energy of the environment you are in. To begin to find research for your own bodily responses I strongly encourage you to actively keep your own records and your own data to see what are your responses.

12 Ways to Start Implementing Interpreting NOW!

- Listen to the music and match your movements to the counts.

- Try moving through the counts instead.

- Dance against the counts.

- Syncopate your moves – going fast for a few moves and then slow down your moves.

- Interact with the space around by using stretch roads or pressing flair. Send your energy out into space. Can you use this physical technique to express your emotions and make choices in the moment of your moving?

- Pretend you are dancing in a box keeping all your movement inside you. Keep your energy circulating in your body. This technique is called *duende* in flamenco and draws those watching you into your space.

- Let the architecture around you inspire your movement choices.

- Find the momentum and give into the momentum of your moves.

- Periodically create an accent through the movement phrase.

- Change the wattage of your dynamic light bulb of energy so one move has 40 watts of intensity and another 100 watts.

- Lose your inner judge: Start by listening to your body as you move without any judgment on your part. This task is much easier than it sounds, but begin with just eight counts of movement and work up to a full movement combination. I tell my students to put their inner judge outside the class and have him sit on a lovely purple stool until the class is over. The point is to work to open your perception of what you are doing as you do it.

- Write to Discover: To broaden your ability to interpret you need to open up your perceptual pathways through giving yourself choices. Okay, now sometimes one doesn't know what one is perceiving until one has captured it and writing is the best way for dancers to document what is being experienced. Try documenting eight counts of your stream of consciousness as you move and see what you are paying attention to. You could also vocally record your experiences with a smart phone audio app.

Integrating Interpreting with Other SPINE strategies

Stretch roads: With interpreting you use moments of suspension, increased lengthening and dynamic alignment as demonstrations of how you are experiencing the moment.
Pressing Flair: Controlling the amount and dynamics of pressing flair adds punctuation and dynamic tone to movement.
Neutralizing Joint Points: Negotiate how much energy to use to create shapes and morph into new ones. Experiment!!
Economizing: Harness the power of speed and lightness to manipulate for communicative and performative purposes.

NEUTRALIZING JOINT POINTS

Warm-up to Neutralizing Joint Points

The language for this fourth SPINE strategy tells you directly how to use this strategy. Start with a joint point. Remember the game connect the dots where you draw lines from dot to dot to create a shape? In this fourth strategy the joints in the body are the dots. Conceiving of these dots as points means that when the points are connected together through sensed tensional relationships a shape is structured by the body. Three joint points need to be connected together by sensing a pulling away from the middle of the body by each joint point to create the tensional relationship between the three joint points.

Neutralize is a key word as to how that tensional relationship occurs. To neutralize is to balance. So the three tensional lines have an equal and opposite sense of tensional pull.

No one joint pulls more than the others.

Neutralizing Joint Points Strategy and Purpose

Strategy: Neutralizing joint points are triangular bonds of equal and counteracting pull between a minimum of three joints during movement.
Purpose: Neutralizing joint points produces whole body integration, stabilization and control for the mover during the constant flux of movement.

Neutralizing joint points (NJP), the fourth SPINE strategy, is all about sensing, creating, and manipulating relationships between the joints of your body. NJP connects to rotation (turnout) making rotation functional for the dancer and not just an aesthetic preference. NJP also establishes torque in the body facilitating all types of turns.

The joints to use for NJP can be any joint in your body, but the most used and the ones you need to sensitize your body to first are: the heels, knees, ASIS/PSIS (these are your anterior superior iliac spine and your posterior superior iliac spine most commonly called your hips); the scapulae, the elbows and the wrists.

I have found the most success with connecting two joints from the supporting side of the body pulling against one joint of the leg or arm that is moving. Connecting two joints on the supporting side of the body to one on the moving side stabilizes your body. Most often I encourage students to imagine the heel and scapula(e) of the supporting side neutralizing against the heel or knee of the working leg. Sometimes you can connect more joints into the imagined neutralized joints and if possible I suggest that you incorporate the elbow or wrist, so that both limbs neutralize to the supporting side.

Herstory of Neutralizing Joint Points

There are many pieces of my training that came together to form neutralizing joint points. First there was the emphasis on the joints in the lower body. The hip, knee, and ankle were constantly worked in a specific relationship with each other. From a variety of teachers I learned that anytime the leg was bent I should be aware of making one joint go back-wards against another joint going forward. For example, in a *cou-de-pieds* position the heel is forward, the knee is back and the hip is forward. The importance played by the joints in the body helped me to clarify the positions of my body as I moved. This forward- back-ward-forward-backwards suggestion went along with considerable attention on the heel as the initiator in leg movement.

The heel was continually framed as the important joint to keep the leg open in turnout. With my hyperextended legs it wasn't until I could perform the ideas of Anne Hebard and let my knee soften coming into a tendu that I began to see the importance of this heel leading the leg movements as important in rotation.

It was Anne Hebard again who one day when as trainees at Harkness everyone was ex-hausted she said to use the joints with an x-ray sensation, if you will. Hebard asked all trainees to think about the bones in the body. She said something to the effect of, "imagine just your bones are moving." As I attempted to imagine my own skeleton doing pliés and battements *tendus*, I found my movements to be much lighter and I was doing more of what I wanted to with my body and using less force in the process.

Over time, I discovered that by applying equal pressure to selected joints throughout my body, I could be aware of my entire body, access my turnout and monitor the changing shapes of my body in different dance techniques. I could immediately access the parts of my body as needed as I changed from rehearsing a Balanchine work in one studio to Lester Horton's *Guernica* in another.

Jazz choreography with all the isolations was easier when I focused on the connected lines of tension created by my joints working one joint against the other in the process. Intuitively, I had developed in my inner technique a connection of the joints to each other to guide my body in and out of shapes that was transferable from one dance genre to another.

The idea of neutralizing I then took a step further. I experimented and found that when I used a joint of the working leg against joints on the supporting leg even greater stability in the position was possible. Two joints on the supporting side against one joint on the working leg kept me on balance consistently.

As I began to do research into my strategy neutralizing joint points I reflected on the use of turnout and how the neutralizing joint points strategy situated turnout in the dancer's own body rather than in an ideal image. In other words neutralizing joint points gave a dancer access to whatever rotation her individual body could produce. My students using neutralizing joint points began to work in their bodies not trying to reproduce ideal bodies. I have consistently found that when dancers of all shapes and sizes with varying degrees of natural rotational capability put neutralizing joint points in action for their own body they discover their turnout as their body can handle it. Teaching neutralizing joint points I've found a dancer's turnout becomes functional and a necessary element to dance technique rather than just an aesthetic ideal serving no purpose.

Applying Herstory to You

You might try exploring how you use your heels as you move. How loud is the voice of your heel as you move? How often do you listen to your heel? The heel is crucial in using NJP and one of the most used joint points so the more you can become aware of the heel the better. The scapula or shoulder blade is another area you might want to question and become more aware of.

A second way is to determine what you sense when you think of only your bones moving. If you find that you are over-recruiting your muscles when you imagine only your bones moving that is an important find. Use the image of only your bones to assist you to access your joints faster.

Neutralizing Joint Points and Healthy Movement

Make Rotation Functional and Keep Your Joints Healthy

With NJP you keep your joints healthy when you work a team of joint points and don't let one joint dictate to the body by over rotating. The knee and the heel are the two joints to watch out for with over rotation. Keep both of these joints connected to two others on the supporting side in a joint point team. I'm not saying that the knee, ankle and hip of the working leg need to be aligned so much as it is that the working knee needs to rotate in conjunction with the scapula and the heel of the opposite side of the body. This across the body support is necessary to access your body's tensegrity as a way to maintain health. Using this across the body support sets up the tensional connections that create an overall tensional integrity in the shape you are creating and create a joint point team.

Neutralized in a joint point team the working knee does not over pull to possibly injure a joint on the supporting side. It's the idea of this joint point team that spans your entire body that for me makes rotation functional. First because you are able to provide the support that is necessary to create, maintain and transition into rotated positions. Second, because you use YOUR rotation and I repeat YOUR rotation (not an ideal rotation, but YOUR rotation) to its fullest.

There are many studies on turnout, but most of them research positions and not how turnout is used to control movement or access the bodily hubs connecting the limbs to the torso at this time. Much more research is needed on functional rotation.

Key into Proprioception and Contribute to Anticipatory Attention

Proprioception is your ability to sense where your body is during movement. When you key into your proprioception you can respond with haste to any stimulus that your body sends out for help. If your proprioception tells you that your weight needs to be more on the left foot, your right elbow needs to extend to balance yourself out, or you need to hop to maintain the vertical- you just do it!

With NJP, because you are heightening your awareness to your joints, you are turning up the volume on your proprioception. You are helping your body find its own balance.

By choosing to focus on joint points that connect the body into one holistic piece, rather than trying to control isolated body parts, you enable what you may think is impossible when it comes to anticipatory awareness and that is reacting to a stimulus before it comes into existence. In other words, your ability to sense your body becomes so finely tuned that you can in advance realize where you need to put your attention next without waiting for your body to send a signal!

I suggest you google proprioception, check out YouTube as well to see for yourself the nervous system at work. Do an image search for proprioceptors can also assist you in understanding proprioception. I suggest you look at the joints specifically as this is where many proprioceptors relay information from to the brain about where your body is in space during movement.

Work YOUR Rotation to Prevent Tissue Overload

YOUR body has a personal amount of rotation from the hips. NJP helps you to find and work with that amount whatever it is in a way that the whole body supports.

Personal turnout is discovered through creating a tensional network of joint points throughout the body that stabilize legs rotating outward. This stabilization of turnout at YOUR limit prevents the tissue overload that is so harmful in over rotation by forcing the legs farther to the side. Realize you have about 60% of the rotation coming from the hips, 15% coming from the knee and the rest from the ankle. These are estimates as everyone's body is different, but they give you an idea of how the leg joints open up to rotate. That is why making joint point connections throughout the torso in the scapula and ASIS/PSIS, elbows and even wrists is so important to prevent forcing one joint in your leg more than your body can support.

In taking the leg bent or extended to the side, connect the heel and/or knee of the lifted leg to the opposite ASIS and opposite scapula in a triangle of NJP. You will feel as a result both the stabilization of the three joint points but also the stretch across the front of the pelvis that signals you are working YOUR turnout!

You might want to look into factors that make your turnout amount different from someone else. I suggest you google: femoral anteversion, femoral retroversion, tibial torsion, bowed legs and/or knock-knees, elastin and collagen in the ligament composition as a start. These will help you to understand that how your femur or leg bone sits in the hip/thigh socket, how your tibia articulates with your femur as well as why the chemical composition of your ligaments can all affect your personal rotation.

Don't Ignore YOUR Rotation

Students who are worried about injuring themselves from forcing the legs to rotate sometimes just ignore rotation altogether. These students simply take the leg out to the side but don't use their personal capacity to rotate the legs to stabilize the movement. Muscle tissue is still over-recruited though. Muscular imbalances can and will occur when you ignore your rotation. The result can still be injury when you ignore your rotation and don't use any and this is just what these students are trying to avoid.

I believe that failing to use rotation is as dangerous as over-rotating. To keep the body working for you and utilizing the good tensional integrity that your body has you must stabilize and support the movements of your limbs with supportive tensional connections in the torso. If you lift your leg to the side without using YOUR rotation to create support from your torso, it's mainly the quadriceps holding the leg up. This inefficiency can cause strains to the inner thigh muscles as has happened in some of my students.

If you fail to include the supporting heel on the joint point team the resultant injury could be an ankle sprain. Ankle anatomy provides stronger support on the inside of the leg (medial side) through the deltoid ligament that is strong and not so elastic. In comparison the lateral or side of the ankle has less support and because of this flexibility ankle sprains can occur. Key into the supporting heel and work the rotation to make it functional. Connect that supporting heel to the scapula on the supporting side and also to some other joint that makes sense for the position you are to make rotation functional. Know that the ankle sprain is the most common injury for dancers. Prevent it with NJP!

I suggest you google ankle sprains and see the anatomical information that is available out there about your body. Google the different joints and see how complex they are and how the muscles do not just go up and down, but twist and are different shapes so that tensional connections are constantly being created.

5 Ways to Neutralize Your Joint Points Now!

The Power of One

Trying to sense all three joint points at once may not happen until you become very sensitive to moving your joints. So, pick one joint point such as the heel or the elbow or knee and then relate this joint you chose to two others in movement. Trial and error, okay?

The Revolving One

Each week, pick a different joint to work on as a place to start your focus on your joints. Your choices are: heel, knee, hip (actually ASIS or PSIS see the glossary for definitions), elbow, wrist, scapula, or for the head the back of the ear. Try to stay conscious of that particular joint for the entire class. Notice that joint in every combination. Ask yourself what joint(s) respond(s) to my selected joint as I move. You might realize that the body has an innate ability to find appropriate support from other joints. You won't have to do so much work to train your body, rather you need to train yourself to listen to your body and use what your body already knows how to do!

Sense Lines of Energy

From the dancer's perspective movement is sensed more in lines than circles. Feedback comes to you as a dancer from the observed perspective, but you need to deal with movement from YOUR perspective. After you sense the joint points imagine lines of beneficial tensional energy connecting the three joint points together to create the stabilizing triangle of NJP. Your body during movement relates to itself via these sensed lines of energy.

Find Opportunity at Every Bend

The fastest way to find joint points will be to bend your limbs. The elbow and knee are thus crucial joint points to make sure you are including in your sensorial field. Remember your body has proprioceptional sensors in many joints in order to sense movement so take advantage of every bend of your arms and legs as opportunities to neutralize your joint point connections.

Seize Your Everyday

You move much more outside of dance than you do in a studio, rehearsal or performance. Seize your everyday movement as a way to sensitize yourself to your joints. When you are sitting at the computer, riding the bike, walking to class or even watching TV do a quick scan of your joints and try to find your whole body triangle tensional relationships. The more you can bring the relationships of your joints into your awareness during everyday movement the stronger the sensations from your joints will be when you are in the studio dancing.

Integrating NJP with other SPINE strategies

Stretch Roads: Neutralize joints in extended positions to steady yourself. In flexed positions the distal aspect of a joint point recycles by elongating into a stretch road.

Pressing Flair: Press into the floor/air to start creating a stretch road from an NJP shape.

Interpreting: Put the brakes on your movement with NJP as a way to interpret, yet retain control through staying connected to the bodily centers (scapular and sacral hubs).

Economizing: Specify where to economize using NJP. Send energy to the distal aspect of the joints to manage movement of the entire appendage quickly and effectively.

ECONOMIZING

Warm-Up to Economizing

The choice of the word economizing for the fifth SPINE strategy refers to the idea of reduction enabling you as a dancer to do more with less. What is being reduced is the amount of effort and where you place that effort. When you reduce the amount of effort you can then become spot specific where you initiate movement from. When you know precisely where you are initiating movement from and this can be multiple places then you are able to move more of your body with less effort. When you can move more of your body by spending less energy speed also comes into the picture. You can move fast and move big. Less effort and less vagueness regarding initiation are the strands of the movement experience packed into the language of economizing.

Economizing Strategy and Purpose

Strategy: Economizing digs deep into the details of movement initiation.
Purpose: Economizing gives you the keys to varying the speed and intensity of your energy during movement.

Your body is no stranger to speed. A nerve impulse travels at approximately 200 miles per hour through your body. But for you as a dancer speed is a unique challenge. How can you move quickly without stressing and tensing your entire body? The key is in the ignition – where your movement starts. It's so important for you to find specific initiation points because while you may not realize this physically, anatomically and definitely biomechanically for the body it makes a huge difference where the movement begins.

The tensional pulls that comprise the framework for the shapes your body makes are created from your choice of where you initiate those pulls in the body. For example, beginning the movement with the elbow will set up different tensional relationships in your body than if you begin it with your wrist. The physical connections, the kinetic relationships, the possibilities for what move is next all come from knowing specifically where to start the movement. The clearer your initiation of the movement the more accurate your body can match the amount of tension you need to maintain your framework with where you are going.

This discovery for me of the connection between quick movement depending on clear initiations reminds me of dancing the jitterbug in Lois Bewley's *Flying Home* piece, where I found that to do the quick footwork and jazzy hands meant I needed to spend time finding out where the movement initiated. I noticed that if I used the farthest point, say the elbow or knee or toe, and operated my limb from there, then the movement felt light while all the time I sensed a groundedness. The lightness that I felt during the movement was important to injury prevention. Lightness is a property of the tensegretic body and if you can feel that lightness as you move you are doing the movement without over recruiting muscles. Chances are that you are working with tensegrity and connecting to your centers as you move quickly.

Take another example: If you think of just lifting your leg to the front, then chances are the quadriceps will take over as they are the largest leg muscle and can handle the job. If you pinpoint your energy to initiate the move instead from your heel and use the stretch roads and pressing flair together your leg will go up, the quadriceps will go along for the ride without exhibiting unnecessary gripping or tension, and you can connect to your center, through your pyramidalis muscle in the pelvic floor. The stretch roads and joint points can then guide you through space as you move and the leg will swiftly move wherever you want it to go. So, being precise and specific about where you begin movements will allow your body to streamline the effort needed to perform them. You keep the kinetic connection to the centers of your body and you can move a lot of your body quickly without harm.

Don't Use a Shovel to Hit a Fly

To economize is to avoid waste or extravagance. Using a shovel to hit a fly is extravagant. Straightening your leg by tensing every muscle in the leg is a waste of your body's energy. The fly can be eliminated with a four-inch flyswatter and your leg can be lifted with much less force and more skill. The skill is economizing. Now realize that economizing doesn't mean that you don't do any work or that you don't sense any effort in your muscles when you move. You do. But the trick is knowing where, when, and how much energy you need. You need to know how to do more with less.

Less is More

I often heard the phrase "less is more" from my directors/teachers when I was dancing. I struggled with what exactly this phrase could mean in terms of my ability to sense movement and direct energy through my body to execute the moves I was asked to do. Here is how that phrase translates into the strategy of economizing.

1. Less intense energy = more energy variability

To understand different intensities of energy in your body imagine a light bulb. Light bulbs are different watts. Exactly as different bulbs have different wattage and, thus different levels of brightness, so too does energy in the body have different intensities and for different reasons. To do a battement tendu to the front might require 40 watts of your energy at a moderate tempo, but it requires even less watts to initiate a tendu when the movement is speeded up. To perform a high kick to the front as the Rockettes do requires maybe 80 watts to start the first kick, and then it reduces to 70 watts for the rest of the kicks in the sequence. So, for speed and repetitive actions economizing means you take into consideration that the intensity of the energy you will need to perform the movement varies.

2. Less initial energy = finding the initiation point(s)

Less here means less initial energy used to start the movement when you are working for speed. If you use say 100 watts of energy and flood that energy into your arms or legs your energy will stop in the upper part of your limb, the biceps/triceps area of the arm or the quadriceps/hamstrings area of the leg. You will become muscle bound and unable to feel the end of your limbs. You will most likely be unable to go from that first movement on to the next without an enormous amount of effort. As a result you won't be able to keep up the movement speed. Please don't misunderstand it's not that it doesn't take effort to move speedily it's that it first takes lightness to find where to initiate and that is one way to theorize the idea of less being more. Less force that you use at the beginning of the movement until you sense the distal body part(s) that you need.

3. Less throwing of energy = more specificity

In this sense less throwing of energy at the entire body and instead knowing where you want to send your energy equals more specificity. You initiate from the right elbow instead of the right arm. You initiate with the left knee instead of the left leg. If you just throw yourself around in movement and lack the   specific places where your body begins a movement then the possibility of injury rises. When you are specific you are able to control your bodily movements with precision because your body finds the appropriate tensional connections and counterbalances.

4. Less time = more bodily control

Moving quickly reduces the size of the movement. You may not see a size difference, but it's felt in the body during movement. You don't say to yourself that you are going to reduce the size of the movement. You do the movement full out. Thus, in your thinking speed cannot cause you to theoretically reduce the movement. What happens is you move fully but the speed with which you are initiating the next move will automatically reduce the space of the movement as much as it needs to be reduced. Let that reduction happen. Let the body take over and control how much of a reduction is needed instead of you dictating to the body before the movement happens.

Experiment: Do a movement of your choice, ask yourself—

What connections do I sense in my body when I do this movement with 100 watts of energy?

How do those connections change when I do this same movement with 40 watts of energy?

If I move as if I were a rag doll doing this movement where do I feel the body sends the energy?

After repeating this movement as a rag doll at least 5 times what sensations persist in my body?

Can I send my energy just to those specific places in my body where it seems my body wants to initiate the movement and then increase my speed without increasing the energy to do the move?

Challenge the Rules

Joanna Kneeland in the 1960s actually filmed the ballet stars of that time and found out that these stars were not following the rules of ballet! Maybe the rule you're trying to follow doesn't work for you either! Remember your body is physically different. You may have to do something extra or take something out of a particular rule in order to find your initiation points. Create your own experiment and challenge the rules!

Think in Multiples

Realize that there might be more than one point of initiation, say the knee and the elbow start this move at the same time. The concept of economizing still applies here. Initiations can and often do occur in multiple places in the body. The clearer you can sense what parts of the body move first the easier it will be for the body to create the necessary counter pulls that will connect you to the center(s) of your movement.

The fuzzier your sensation of what part of the body you need to activate, the heavier the movement will feel, the more effort you will need to expend doing it. Remember lightness is a property of the tensegretic body. So, sensing yourself doing less effort, feeling light or buoyant in the body is also possible. You will also sense yourself grounded at the same time as you sense the light feeling, but the groundedness will most likely be sensed as being far away from where you are sensing the lightness. Sensing groundedness by using pressing flair is not the same thing as sensing over-recruitment. Over-recruitment is felt as a heavy sensation of the moving body. You lose specificity with over-recruitment. Sensing multiple initiation points to economize thus means you use pressing flair to ground yourself realizing that multiple initiation points are possible.

Experiment: Divide and Conquer

How do you figure out where your body starts a move? You experiment with that move. You may know where you're supposed to start, but are you really doing what you're supposed to do? Experiment. Divide the movement up and conquer the initiation points.

When dancing unique, innovative steps trial and error is the preferred way to find the best initiation point. Divide the step into sequences and then you can conquer the initiations. Go slowly at first until your body has a chance to follow what it is you want to do and then you can gradually speed the movements up once you've found the initiation point(s).

Herstory of Economizing

The strategy of economizing revolves around speed and how to make things happen very quickly in the body without hurting oneself. And in my dance experience, the unique problem of speedy movement came when performing Balanchine choreography. In rehearsing and performing Balanchine's *Concerto Barrocco, Donizetti Variations* and the "Russian Girl" in *Serenade* I moved my limbs great distances in just one count.

One count – no big deal right? Except that one count was every one count. The only way to be able to move at that speed without injury I found was to allow all the energy to drain out of the limb, find the most distal part of the limb that you need to move and then initiate the movement with that most distal part.

Take the "chicken step" in *Concerto Barrocco* for example: you step forward on one leg swing the other around to the front and twist your arms and upper body in the opposite direction from the leg swing, and then do the same on the next count in the opposite direction. Using economizing I stepped forward on one leg, sent no energy through my arms and back leg, found the fingertips of both hands and the heel of the leg that was in back and then swung the heel in one direction and the fingertips in the other. All the rest of my body just went along for the ride. By that I mean I didn't direct my body or place other parts of my body anywhere else; just the fingertips of both hands and the heel of the moving leg. Those parts of my body were the only ones I moved. Everywhere else in the body disappeared in my consciousness. I found my points of initiation and then moved them where they needed to go again and again and again. I found if I tensed anywhere it was all over.

Vaganova training also helped me understand speed. As I read and experimented on my own in the summers when I gave myself class to stay in shape I would go through the Vaganova technique doing the classes from books. I noticed how the classes had a progression in speed for the *battement tendu* through the grades. At the most advanced grades a single *tendu* was performed in half of a count.

To execute this brisk *battement tendu*, I had to send what felt like on the inside a thin concentrated stream of energy directly to my heel. I found that if I just plunged the energy into my entire leg it wouldn't work. The energy would clog up my leg and stop at what felt like it was the knee causing the tendu to be initiated more from the quadriceps rather than the heel.

I had a great leap of understanding about the tendu also from the late Joe Duell, from New York City Ballet, when he came to set his ballet *Jubilee* on us in Cincinnati Ballet. During one of his guest morning technique classes he said, "Put your brain in your foot." For some reason that statement clicked. By imagining myself putting my brain in my foot, somehow I found I could move my leg in a *tendu* with lightning speed.

And the last part in this economizing strategy fell into place working with Larry Long in Chicago when I was with Chicago Ballet. I can still hear Larry Long screaming, "less is more!" These three words were favorites of his as he coached me in the role of Sugar Plum Fairy for Ruth Page's *Nutcracker* in the Arie Crown Theatre in Chicago. I would often reflect on these three words trying to fully understand the implications of them. Efficiency was at the heart of the message, I got that, but how did that translate to how I worked inside my body? It was really only when I started to teach at Southern Ballet Theater that I really figured out how best to put all these ideas together and formulate an inclusive economizing strategy.

Applying Herstory to You

Why not try to do a familiar warm-up movement in less time? If you usually take 2 counts to do a movement try doing it in 1 count. If you do this movement in 1 count try splitting that one count and do the movement in a half of a count.

Economizing and Healthy Movement

Break the Habit of Over-recruiting

Using more energy than is necessary to execute a move is over-recruiting. In terms of your muscle tissue over-recruiting in a broad sense that means that you are using for example 1000 muscle fibers to perform a movement that could easily be done with just 100 fibers. When you develop the habit of over-recruiting your muscle tissue cells increase in size making the size of the muscles bigger.

So, instead of sensing bunchiness in muscles as you move, with economizing you sense the muscles as longer and leaner. Sensing and creating muscle length assists with keeping the muscle tissue healthier, leaner and better able to perform the moves needed in dance.

There is a lot of information out there on muscle recruitment and muscle fibers. You might also try motor end plate as this is the neuromuscular connections. Try googling those terms to find out more about how you recruit your muscular effort.

Distinguish between Effort and Force

Effort is needed in dance. Force is not. Effort is the expenditure of energy that is required to move. Force means you're overdoing it.

Economizing allows you to expend energy where and when it is necessary rather than just putting as much effort as you can into a move just to get it done.

With effort the body understands there will be an initial contraction of muscle tissue and then somewhere along the way a release so the process can continue.

With force there is contraction period and that's it. Like holding your breath, you hold your muscle in a contraction. The body thus has to outsource, if you will, to other muscles that normally might not be required to perform this move.

With effort you are working with the processes your body regulates and operates under. With force you are overloading and stressing muscle tissue in a way that is unnecessary and unhealthy over time.

You might want to find out about muscle contractions. There are traditionally three kinds of contractions: isometric, eccentric and concentric. Google these terms to find the differences. You might also want to look at word meanings to get clearer on the distinction between effort and force. Look up these definitions and see how sometimes you need to define your language in order to clarify your understanding.

Breathe

When you breathe you are allowing tensegrity to create counterbalances and the contract/release of the body via muscles and breathing all takes place. The processes in your body are working for you.

When you hold your breath all these body processes become disabled and the body fights through force and over-recruitment to perform the moves you want to do.

Keep breathing, use economizing and your body keys into the tensegretic responses for movement that the body can sustain.

The results you find in Googling "breathing" can be quite informative. Look at YouTube videos and diagrams to really understand the process of taking a single breath!

4 Ways to Implement Economizing NOW!

Count the Ways You Can Mess Up

When you need to move quickly one tendency many dancers have is to freeze and not do anything. Breath is held and panic can set in. Confront your fears of speed by allowing yourself to mess up. Allow yourself to fail. Try making a game of it and counting how many ways you can mess up. Say to yourself: It doesn't matter if my legs get tangled and I can't remember what is next: It doesn't matter if I make a fool of myself. And if you are in a situation where it does matter, then take yourself to a more secluded place and breathe, working through the movement sequence step-by-step getting one movement connected to another and then add another one on until you have the entire phrase.

Boomerang

The way to use economizing is to be able to send your energy to the distal ends of your limbs and work your limbs from the fingertips or heel. If the limbs are bent, then use the elbow or knees instead. Send a thin, laser beam of energy in your imagination to your heel or your fingertips leaving the rest of your limb softened, not completely relaxed, but not fully tensed either. Use just enough energy until you can sense the heel or the fingertips, elbow or knee. Then once you have found these distal ends of your limbs imagine the energy boomeranging back to the connections in your torso. With the boomerang visualization you sense the support coming from the torso for your movement. You can then sense the stretch roads through the limb because you now have sensed the distal end.

When you send the energy to the distal end linearly without boomeranging back to sense the body's support you can't move quick and light. Sensing this process takes some time. Be patient! Practice outside the studio at home with loose limbs and keep breathing until you can achieve this boomerang sensation in a nanosecond.

Play with Spots

The idea here is to play with spots on your body as different initiation points. Outside of class where you feel less stress to perform without error, initiate moves with your elbow and see what sensations you feel in the rest of your body as a result of your elbow initiation. Then try the knee and see what sensory response or tugs in your body that you receive. The point is that if you wait until you are in the studio doing a class or in a rehearsal performing moves you are under pressure and will not have this playful way of approaching your movement. So, when you can play with initiating movement from different places on your body and see what the physical reactions you have are. Through this type of experimentation you will slowly break through the neuromuscular patterning and the motor patterns that are habits to you at the moment. You can only break through or retrain by this type of playful experimentation forcing yourself into a new system is not your best option.

Take a Break

If you are musclebound, have bigger muscles than you would like, and are trying to move quickly, you cannot. Your body needs to lose the muscle tissue.

Take a break from dancing. I've told this to many dancers who after spring semester ask me what can help them over the summer. I say stop dancing – do other physical activities, but stop dancing so that you lose the muscle tissue through atrophy. It's not about weight! I'm not writing that you need to lose weight, you need to let your muscle tissue atrophy a bit so you can build movement habits differently! Then you can then find that sliver of energy to use economizing. Take a break! You deserve it!

Integrating Economizing with other SPINE Strategies

Stretch Roads: Economizing directs the fully extended stretch roads when the dancer needs efficient movement done quickly.
Pressing Flair: Pressing flair finds the distal ends of the limbs so you can use economizing.
Interpreting: Economizing allows the dancer to create a light approach to movement. Economizing can assist in playing with rhythms and creating varied dynamics.
Neutralizing Joint Points (NJP): With increased sensitivity to the joint points economizing can then find specific initiation points faster and with less expended energy.

GLOSSARY

In this section of the book I provide you with the terms that I use in the book for which you might need further explanation.

Active Balance
A technical element of movement: This skill requires one to negotiate to achieve and maintain balance. Balance is not static, but rather an active negotiation accomplished by the body through counterbalances that strategies like stretch roads and pressing flair help to find and bring into the dancer's awareness.

Anticipatory Attention
The idea that a dancer because she is connected to the process of her movement can anticipate where to place her attention next during movement on the way to achieving her movement goal. Stretch roads and neutralizing joint points help greatly by giving the dancer a mapping system of her body and by clearly defining connections between the joints of the body in movement.

Bodily Central Hubs
There are two bodily central hubs – one hub where each scapula connects to the physical spine and a second hub where the sacrum connects to the physical spine. The limbs connect to the physical spine through these two bodily central hubs.

Central Muscular Activation
The idea that movement is activated by connecting to the center of the body. My question to you is: Are you ready to consider that the physical center of the body is the physical spine???

Complimentary Opposites
The inclusive idea of opposites having simultaneous existence rather than cancelling each other out. BOTH up AND down, BOTH right AND left, BOTH front AND back are sensed in the body during movement. Consider the idea that the experience of the mover

is the experience of complimentary opposites in action. Sensing complimentary opposites is the first step to working the body's tensegrity.

Connective Tissue
There are differing opinions on what is included and excluded in connective tissue. Some believe connective tissue is just fascia in the body. Others consider connective tissue to be the tissue involved in the musculo-skeletal system but not the bones. The SPINE strategies approach the definition of connective tissue such that: bones, muscles, fascia, ligaments, tendons, and cartilage are all connective tissue. The reason is that all these tissues grow out of each other and from the perspective of the body all these tissues are connected.

Core
An ambiguous term meaning anything from the abdominal region to a six-pack to the torso's stabilizing muscles. The term core is not used in the SPINE strategies because of this ambiguity. Instead central bodily hubs is used to be specific about where the limbs connect to the physical spine and create the body's center.

Crossed-Extensor Reflexes
A reflex relying on the contralaterality of the body to withdraw from dangerous stimuli. In stepping on a sharp object the weight shifts to the contralateral foot so the other foot can withdraw from the sharp object.

Dynamic Alignment
This is a concept for technique addressing alignment in 21st century dance as relational, omnidirectional, and accomplished via counterbalance. Verticality is no longer the only or most important option in positioning the body. Alignment in the moving body is dynamic not positioned.

Economizing
The fifth strategy in the SPINE: Economizing allows you to move quickly by connecting the tips of the appendages to the bodily central hubs. You feel light, quick and connected as you move with speed.

Extension
Extension is one possible movement outcome for the joints in the body.

Extending is the opposite of flexion or bending a limb or joint in the body. To extend means to go in the direction of a straight line with a body shape.

Exteroception
Exteroception is one of the perceptual pathways in the body. Exteroception brings the

outside in to the body. Exteroception deals with perceiving the environment, and other bodies in that environment. Exteroception is focused by attention that increases the awareness of what is outside the dancer's body during movement.

Fascia

Fascia is connective tissue in the body that is currently being researched while it used to be just thrown away by anatomists. Most recent findings are that fascia is alive and has neural cells embedded in the tissue that assist with bodily communication. Somatic practitioner Mary Bond calls the fascia "the body's internet." Sometimes during stretch roads, pressing flair or neutralizing joint points the connections and tensional pulls you sense are indications of your fascial connections.

Flexion

Flexion means bending. The arms flex, legs flex and spine flexes as well as the fingers, toes, wrists, and other joints. Flexion of joints in movement is when these joints are most vulnerable because ligaments that guide the bones articulating often go lax; thus, increasing the importance of sensing neutralizing joint points when your joints flex. With NJP you create a whole body network to reintegrate any lost ligamental structures by flexing a particular joint.

Functional Rotation

Dance in the 21st Century must redefine turnout as rotation to include all the various permutations of turning the legs in, out and combinations of these. Rotation then must become a whole body event so that rotation is functional contributing to bodily control, maintaining kinetic connections to bodily centers, and assisting with creating and dissolving of bodily shapes. Neutralizing joint points is the strategy to help discover for yourself your own functional rotation.

Hyperextension

Joints that when extended can go beyond 180°. Hyperextended knees are common as are hyperextended elbows and thumbs. Sensing how to work with hyperextended joints can require the dancer to reconceive of energy pathways and what connections are related and which ones are not.

Interoception

The neural pathways in the body that deliver information continuously to the brain on the internal organs, i.e. breathing, heartbeat, pain, core temperature, and any other visceral issues. This internal monitoring never stops, but is only brought to conscious attention when action is needed because normal limits have been surpassed.

Interpreting

The third SPINE strategy: Interpreting connects performance skills to technical study of bodily movement by demonstrating how the dancer can utilize different facets of bodily perception to make choices in the moment of movement.

Joint Health

Keeping joints healthy is vital to injury prevention and prolonging a dance career. Maintaining muscular balance so that the joint is not pulled more when one set of muscles contract than the other is one way to keep joints healthy.

Massage, attention to trigger points, and other bodywork remedies can also assist you in maintaining joint health. If one set of muscles is weaker around a particular joint, then weight training can help to strengthen that set of muscles. Usually a physical therapist or personal trainer can assist you in developing a program to balance your muscles, but daily you can address trigger points.

Kinesthesia

The ability to sense yourself moving. Kinesthesia feels like stretching; sensing the tugs and pulls of the muscles as they move and the weight of your body as you move as well.

The more you listen to your body the more you are aware of not just the moving part, but how the rest of the body is responding to the creation and dissolution of positions. A sophisticated kinesthesia means that you are able to really be specific as to where in your body you move and that you do not clutter your sense of motion with force but operate your body with specificity.

Neuromuscular Patterning

The ability of the body to remember movement through the motor pattern located in the brain. It's the brain that remembers movement – not the muscles! Neuromuscular patterning refers to the way you perform a movement: where you initiate, what type of effort you use, details on the positioning of your bodily parts, all information on that movement is contained in neuromuscular patterning of which the blueprint is filed in the brain. There is no such thing as muscle memory! The muscle tissue cannot support remembering! All muscle tissue can do is contract!!! Neuromuscular patterning is stored in the brain in motor patterns.

Neutralizing Joint Points (NJP)

The fourth SPINE strategy: What is neutralized is the amount of push or pull that you apply to all three or more joints in a position so that the force on each joint feels neutral when compared with the other two joint points. No one joint is pushed farther back than the other. This particular strategy connects to functional rotation and creating torque for turns.

Organization of the Body
For the dancer, the arrangement of the bones, muscles and other connective tissues in the body. The practicality of how these tissues are put together needs to coincide with theoretical models used by the dancer so there is more efficient and healthy movement. Throughout this book the organization of the body is conceived as a whole entity, a tensegretic structure where movement of one part affects the whole. Organization of the body comes from considering the entire body and not just bodily parts moving.

Osteoarthritis
A condition of inflammation in the joints. This inflammation occurs due to a change in the integrity of the joint that is most often caused by a lessening in the space between the bones in the joint. When the bones most often through muscular imbalances start to come closer together the joint becomes inflamed. Pain, swelling occurs. Usually this condition does not occur until a person is past middle age, however there is much the dancer can do to prevent this condition during their career. Weight training for muscular endurance to prevent overuse of muscle tissue, regular bodywork to reduce tense, tight muscles, and attention to working the body tensegretically are prevention methods for osteoarthritis.

Over-Recruitment of the Muscles
Dancers over-recruit muscular tissue through forcing bodily positions or gripping. Physically what over-recruitment does is call upon more muscle fibers than is necessary to perform movement. Muscles gripping can also occur in a static contraction when the body is not counterbalanced effectively. Over-recruitment of the muscle tissue can become a habit that does not help with flow, grace, or healthy movement.

Patellofemoral Syndrome
A condition where bending the knee hurts. The pain comes from the patella not going up and down to track, but rather having a muscular imbalance where the side of the leg (iliotibial band) is stronger than the inside of the leg (inner thighs). When this imbalance occurs bending the knee brings the kneecap to the side instead of staying in place. This pull causes the pain. See a doctor, get a physical therapist to give you a regime of stretching to rebalance and keep this condition in check.

Perceptual Pathways
The three pathways discussed in this book are: interoception, exteroception, and proprioception. Each pathway is self-contained such that information traveling along the interoceptive pathway does not change to the exteroceptive. Identifying what occurs on your perceptual pathways through writing and self-reporting can be of great assistance in gathering information on your process of attention; specifically, finding where and when you place your attention, and how does that attention move as you are moving is useful to healthful movement.

Pressing Flair
The second SPINE strategy that many of my students feel helps with whole body integration because it unlocks the tensegretic response for them. You press into the floor and you press into the air in order to sense resistance as you move.

Proprioception
Proprioception is the name of the body's system for knowing where all body parts are in space so that balance through counterbalance can be maintained in movement. The brain does not see; rather, one way the brain monitors balance is through tinkering with the signals sent to the brain from the proprioceptors. The proprioceptors are located in the muscles and joints and send signals to the brain on the tension that is used during movement. Keying into proprioception through attention to muscular length (stretch roads) and the joints (NJP) help you to tag along these bodily processes already inbuilt so you can move in a healthful manner.

Pyramidalis
The pyramidalis is a muscle in the shape of a pyramid located at the lowest point of the rectus abdominus. When the pyramidalis is contracted you activate a connection into the linea alba (strong fibrous line in the front center of the body) and you can connect into the transverse abdominis. The sequence is important to engage this muscle you must start in the pubic area and work from the bottom up to the navel and into the center of the body. Contracting the center (around the navel) first disables this connection. Connecting and reconnecting in movement to the pyramidalis means that the legs stay connected to the sacral hub as you move.

Quadratus Lumborum
A muscle that connects the ribs to the pelvis and is very important to creating and sensing length in the torso while keeping the spine, rib, and pelvis connected. The Latin name tells you that this muscle is somewhat square and is in the lumbar region. Its actual point of origin is the posterior iliac crest and it inserts into the 12th rib and the transverse processes of the lumbar in vertebrae 1-4. You lengthen this muscle through sending the navel into the center of body and letting the ribs hang. If you stick the ribs out the quadratus lumborum is not activated.

Righting Reflexes
Righting reflexes are a group of reflexes that help to balance the body. Relying only on the optic reflex is not enough. Vestibular reflexes from the inner ear as well as head and neck reflexes work together to keep the body in a moving balance. These are the righting reflexes – the ones that keep you upright.

Serape Effect

A serape is a Mexican shawl. In the body, contralaterality occurs as a result of the contraction of a set of four muscles that connect the spine via the scapula to the ribs and to the pelvis working from the back to the front of the body in the shape of the serape. The four muscles that comprise this kinetic connection are: rhomboids (going from the spine to the scapula), serratus anterior (a muscle going from the scapula to the ribs on the front of the body), internal obliques (taking the connection across the abdominal area), external obliques (taking the connection to the pelvis). Utilizing the serape effect during *pirouettes* one twists in the torso and keys into a set of connections already set up in the body allowing one to move in a healthful manner.

Simultaneous Synergistic Organization

A concept emphasizing that movement comes from cooperation and coordination between muscles. No one muscle is responsible for a movement. Muscles work as a community together to move.

Somatics

A field that is still defining itself. The somatic field concerns the primacy of the body and what the experience of the process of moving entails. In this book, somatics refers to the dancer's ability to be more fully aware of movement from the body's perspective. Somatics is not about rules or enforcing an aesthetic position, but rather turns to processes of discovery and exploration to develop an attuned individual mover who knows her body through experiencing movement.

Structure of the Body

The body is made to move, thus the structure of the body is one where tissues grow out of each other and adapt to movement. The muscle tissue grows out of the bone, the tendon grows out of the muscle tissue and into the bone. This unified structure means that the dancer in order to move the body effectively and in a healthy manner needs to continually reinforce the idea of unity and whole body. The structure of the body during movement means that the experience of the dancer or technique from the dancer's viewpoint is center stage in the studio.

Synaptic Facilitation

Also called neural facilitation, synaptic facilitation is the ability of the body to make movement easier when that same movement is repeated. The repetition along a similar route of neurons in the body over time means that the body learns this particular route. Over time the same move will get easier and easier. Synaptic facilitation is why repeating a move efficiently and effectively over time increases your ability to perfect that move. However, when trying to relearn how to do a particular move synaptic facilitation is what makes this relearning difficult as well. Relearning means you need to break up the synaptic facilitation.

A somatic approach is best when trying to relearn so that you interrupt the synaptic facilitation and allow the body to discover new neural routes.

Tensegrity

I came upon the word tensegrity when I was researching the body at university. Tensegrity is a compound word joining tension and integrity. The word was coined by the architect Buckminster Fuller after he saw the work of Kenneth Snelson a visual artist who had created the Needle Tower a vertical structure built from rods and tensile wire. Tensegrity describes a structure where the forces of push and pull are joined in a win-win relationship. Both forces are present and both forces together create a structure that can in a sense defy gravity. By that I mean that instead of having to put one stone on top of another to build a vertical structure, verticality can be created via zigzags that occur through tensional relationships where both push and pull are present. A tennis racket, a balloon, a bicycle wheel and a geodesic dome are all tensegretic structures. As it turns out so is the human body.

Donald E. Ingber, American cell biologist and bioengineer at the Wyss Institute at Harvard, wrote in the *Scientific American* that tensegrity was present in both the micro and macro organization of the human body. In the musculo-skeletal system he describes tensegrity as "the 206 bones that constitute our skeleton are pulled up against the force of gravity and stabilized in a vertical form by the pull of tensile muscles, tendons and ligaments." Viewing the musculo-skeletal system as a tensegrity is a new way of modeling how the body is put together for the medical community.

Orthopedic surgeon Dr. Stephen Levin has also written extensively about the body as a structure of tensional integrity. It turns out he, too, was inspired by Kenneth Snelson's tensegretic sculpture, The Needle Tower. Dr. Levin believes this new model is a result of the new materials used to build buildings. The new materials allow architects and visual artists to create structures where tensional relationships create the shape of the structure and also the integrity of the structure rather than just putting one brick on top of another as society did to build the pyramids and Greek temples.

Putting one brick on top of another is a model that has been around in dance for a long time for alignment of the body. I certainly had teachers who told me to put one bone on top of another for good alignment. But while one bone on top of another may be what the body looks like from the viewer's perspective, placing one bone on top of another is not the reality of what a dancer does, nor how a dancer feels when producing good alignment. Nor is one bone on top of another connected to the physicality of what is really happening in the body. In a healthy body one bone doesn't touch another and if it does then you are in pain and have a problem that can escalate to requiring surgical intervention.

Thus, tensegrity is a progressive model for the whole body.

Transverse Abdominis (TA)

The deepest of the abdominal muscles. This muscle can be disabled through doing too many sits-ups. The transverse abdominis muscle is strengthened through use and this use does not include sit-ups or crunches of any kind. TA muscle use comes from finding the pubic area and using the pyramidalis first to engage the transverse abdominis. The sequence of engagement is important because if you just contract the abdominals you will not always engage the TA. The TA is the inner corset that supports the back. It's not the muscle that creates the "six-pack." Its origin is in the iliac crest and thoracolumbar aponeurosis along the internal surface of the costal cartilages 7-12. It is this connection to the thoracolumbar aponeurosis and the ribs that makes the muscle run horizontally and contrary to other abdominal muscles. The transverse abdominis inserts into the abdominal aponeurosis and linea alba and pubis. Thus the transverse abdominis connects the back, ribs and pelvis together and is a crucial muscle to finding the lower bodily center that so many people popularly refer to as the core.

Turnout

A traditional dance term now outdated in the 21st century. Turnout refers solely to the rotation of the legs outward. In 21st century dance, there are many more options and a definite need to theorize turnout as a whole body event. Functional rotation is a better term for this concept.

Whole Body Integration

An element of most techniques where all limbs in the body are connected to each other via their kinetic chain of connections to the physical spine. The moving body achieves a unified whole during movement. Sensation of the whole body as integrated is not that one senses the entire body all the time during movement, but that one senses connections and relationships that designate to the mover where the bodily centers are. The mover using whole body integration has options and can control movement in a healthy manner. All SPINE strategies can assist you in sensing and creating whole body integration.

CPSIA information can be obtained
at www.ICGtesting.com
Printed in the USA
LVOW02s0001200617

538695LV00001B/13/P